Betty Crocker's

PASTA

COOKBOOK

MACMILLAN • USA

MACMILLAN

A Simon & Schuster Macmillan Company
1633 Broadway
New York, NY 10019-6785

Library of Congress Cataloging-in-Publication Data
Crocker, Betty

[Betty Crocker's Pasta cookbook]
Betty Crocker's pasta cookbook.

p.   cm.

Includes index.
ISBN 0-02-860374-5 (acid-free paper)

1. Cookery (Pasta)   I. Title.

TX809.M17C763   1995
641.8'22—dc20   95-12564
`CIP

GENERAL MILLS, INC.

Betty Crocker Food and Publications Center

Director: Marcia Copeland
Editor: Lori Fox
Recipe Development: Altanette Autry, Nancy Cooper, Cathy Swanson
Food Stylists: Kate Courtney Condon and Cindy Lund

Nutritionists: Elyse A. Cohen, M.S., and Nancy Holmes, R.D.

Photographic Services
Photographer: Nanci Doonan Dixon

Cover by Iris Jeromnimon
Designed by Michele Laseau

For consistent baking results, the Betty Crocker Food and
Publications Center recommends Gold Medal flour.

Manufactured in the United States of America
10 9 8 7 6 5 4 3 2 1
First Edition

Cover: Chorizo Ravioli with Roasted Red Pepper Cream (page 70), Back cover: Pasta Torte Slices (page 42), Fresh Pasta (pages 19–21),
Chocolate Chip-Pecan Shells with Caramel Sauce (page 37),
Title Page: Baked Ravioli (page 30)

NTRODUCTION

We know what everyone loves—pasta! Everyone is on the lookout for great new pasta recipes; no one ever seems to have enough. Betty Crocker has "oodles-of-noodles" for pasta fans everywhere, with more than 185 tempting recipes that bring you pasta like you've never had it before!

These make-me recipes use either fresh or dry pasta, whichever suits you best. Sample Garden Gazpacho Pasta Salad, Fusilli with Smoked Salmon, Teriyaki Beef Stir-fry, Spicy Peanut Butter-Pork Pasta and other delicious meal ideas.

Feeling adventurous? Then you'll enjoy the chapter on making pasta from scratch, starting with a simple basic pasta, then moving to delightful flavored pastas, such as Mushroom-Leek Pasta and Cheese-Pepper Pasta. You'll love being able to personalize your pasta and create wonderful taste sensations whenever you please.

Did you think pasta was only for a main meal? Surprise! We've included recipes for unexpectedly delicious appetizers—Crispy Chili Twists, Tangy Bacon-Topped Tortellini—and even pasta desserts. Everyone will love Chocolate Chip-Pecan Shells with Caramel Sauce, Cherry-Streusel Lasagna and the other enticing desserts here.

We've included a pasta glossary, an easy-to-use pasta identification photo, tips on cooking times and other information to be sure your pasta is perfect. Plus there are great ideas for easy bottled sauce fix-ups, low-fat sauces and even instructions for a pasta party. This is truly one-stop pasta shopping!

We think you'll be in pasta heaven with this complete round-up of wonderful pasta recipes. With recipes for pasta with meat, poultry, seafood, meatless pastas and pasta salads, plus appetizer pastas, dessert pastas, sensational sauce ideas and pasta pointers, you'll have a pasta adventure with Betty Crocker!

Betty Crocker

CONTENTS

PASTA PRIMER

Pasta used to mean spaghetti, lasagna or noodles, but now it is so much more! From dried to fresh, short to long, curly to ridged and flat to tubular, the tremendous variety available is certainly worth exploring.

To help guide you through the plethora of enticing "pastabilities," we've identified the historical origins and names given to particular varieties. Like most Italian foods, pasta names have specific meanings representative of the shape or the intended use for preferred dishes. Despite similarity in shape, some varieties were originally referred to by different names depending on regional traditions.

PASTA GLOSSARY

Acini de pepe: This quick-cooking, tiny peppercorn-shaped pasta is perfect in soups, salads and side dishes. When cooked, it swells up to roughly twice the size of the uncooked pasta.

Bucatini: A long, hollow noodle, thicker than spaghetti, that originated in Naples. *Bucato* literally means "with a hole." When broken into thirds and served with a sauce, this noodle will absorb the flavor inward, adding more flavor to each bite.

Cannelloni (Manicotti): A large, 4-inch tubular noodle that is usually stuffed and baked. Derived from the word *canna,* it means "hollow cane."

Capellini (Angel Hair): *Capellini* means "thin hair" and is one of the thinnest cut spaghetti noodles. Legend has it that Parmesan cheese clings to this pasta like gold clings to angel's hair. It is a very quick pasta to prepare as it needs to boil only a few minutes and is best served with light sauces and in soups.

Cellophane Noodles: Also called bean threads because the starch they are made from comes from the green mung bean. These dried, translucent noodles must be presoaked before use in most recipes unless they are added directly to soups or simmering liquids. The dry noodles can also be deep-fried and puff up instantly and dramatically to a size many times larger than when dry. The deep-fried noodles are crunchy and as light as air.

Couscous ("koos-koos"): The most tiny pasta, it is a staple of North African and some Middle Eastern cuisines. Couscous plays a dual role. It is actually granular semolina, as pasta is made from, but is most often used in place of rice. Couscous is available in regular and precooked varieties. Precooked couscous cooks in just 5 minutes.

Ditali or Ditalini: A pasta cut into short segments resembling thimbles, with ditali being a little bit wider. Two types are available: lisci or smooth, which is appropriate for soups and salads; and regati, meaning grooved, which is suitable for chunky sauces. Typically it is cooked in soups or served with a vegetable sauce.

Egg Roll Wrappers: Also known as wonton wrappers, these are made of flour, eggs and salt. Although these wrappers contain the same ingredients found in egg pasta, they are not considered pasta in the traditional sense. But these convenient little squares work well for a variety of fillings such as in our recipe for Sausage-Mushroom Pasta Calzones on page 68.

Elbow Macaroni: A short, curved, tubular-shaped pasta. This pasta is used extensively in casseroles and salads.

Farfalle (Bow Ties): A bow-tie-shaped pasta. Traditionally, this pasta is accompanied by colorful sauces, reminiscent of blooming gardens, with fresh herbs or ripe vegetables such as sweet bell peppers or zucchini. Miniature bow ties are known as *tripolini,* which is appropriate for soups or salads.

Fettuccine: Literally meaning "little strands," fettuccine is a long, flat noodle, usually 1/4 inch wide. Thick, smooth white sauces, such as Alfredo, cling beautifully to this pasta. Fettuccine is available in many flavors including plain and spinach.

Fusilli: A long or short curled pasta from southern Italy usually served with spicy tomato sauces. Hailing originally from Naples, it is also known as *eliche*, or "propellers," for its quality of trapping particles of the sauce and propelling them between the palate and the tongue.

Gnocchi: Any of several soft dumplings made from boiled potatoes, eggs and flour. Gnocchi means "lumps," due to the irregular, somewhat craggy shapes these dumplings have when cooked in soups. They range from marble to golf ball size, and are boiled and served with a butter or cream based sauce. Although gnocchi isn't pasta in the traditional sense, it tastes like pasta and is often used like a pasta, so we've included it in this book.

Lasagna: These noodles are flat and about 2 inches wide with either ruffled or straight edges. The classic Italian casserole called lasagna is made by layering cooked noodles with a red sauce and variety of cheeses and then baking. Frozen, precooked sheets (not cut) of lasagna noodles are available.

Linguine: A flat, thin noodle served with light sauces such as clam or pesto. The name means "little tongues," as its original shape resembled the thickness of a song bird's tongue.

Mafalde: This is a long, flat, narrow noodle with curled edges, popular for sauces with seafood. Mafalde is also available in a short length and is often referred to as mini-lasagna noodles.

Mostaccioli: A short cut pasta about 2 inches long. These tubular "mustaches" have slanted cuts at both ends. Mostaccioli can have a smooth or grooved finish.

Noodles: Noodles can be fresh, frozen or dry and made with or without eggs. This flat pasta comes in a variety of lengths and widths, including: extrawide, wide, medium, fine, ribbons and dumpling.

Novelty Pasta: Fun, funky new pasta shapes and flavors are popping up in gourmet food stores everywhere. You can get pasta in the shape of one of our fifty states, trees, animals, foods and objects such as grape clusters and stars. Often these shapes are available seasonally and include Christmas trees, bunny rabbits and hearts. Beyond these shapes, you can find some uniquely flavored pasta too—how about Cabernet Sauvignon or Chardonnay?

Penne: A short cut pasta about 1 1/4 inches long. Tubular in shape with slanted cuts at both ends, penne can have a smooth or grooved finish; it is narrower than mostaccioli. The word *penne* means "feather," indicating either the lightness of the noodle or the transversally cut shape that resembles a wing of a bird. It is excellent with tomato and vegetable sauces.

Radiatore: Also known as pasta nuggets, this pasta is shaped like car radiators. This ruffled little pasta is an excellent choice for light sauces and salads because the ruffles can catch all the flavors in the sauce or dressing.

Ramen: These are instant, deep-fried noodles that cook in about five minutes. They are most often sold in cellophane bags and include a seasoning packet and dehydrated vegetables. The noodles can be used dry, as a crunchy addition to salads or cooked. Some brands bake rather than deep-fry the noodles and are lower in fat.

Ravioli: Pillow-shaped pasta popular in several Italian regions, usually made with a stuffing of spinach and cheese. Ravioli are also filled with ingredients such as crabmeat or pumpkin. Traditionally served with butter or Parmesan, this pasta is also delicious with tomato and meat sauces. Due to its richness, ravioli is usually served as a main course or on special occasions.

Rice Noodles: These are made from rice flour and water and are translucent. Rice noodles come in many forms from fresh to dried. Dried rice noodles are the most widely available and are usually in the form of very thin strands. These noodles must be presoaked before use in most recipes unless they are added directly to soups or simmering liquids. The dry noodles can also be deep-fried and puff up instantly and dramatically to a size many times larger than when dry. The deep-fried noodles are crunchy and as light as air.

Rigatoni: Short cut, wide tubular pasta with lengthwise grooves, about 1 inch long. It suits most chunky sauces and meat sauces.

Rosamarina (Orzo): So named for its resemblance to rice, this pasta is ideal in soups, salads and side dishes.

Rotini: A short cut pasta with a corkscrew shape that is sold plain or tricolored. A wider version of this shape is called rotelle. Rotini is a favorite for pasta salads.

Soba: Made from buckwheat and is brown in color; it tastes similar to whole wheat pasta. Soba noodles originate from Japan.

Shells: Shells are available in jumbo, medium and small sizes. Jumbo shells are great stuffed, while medium and small shells are more suited for thick sauces, soups and salads.

Spaghetti: Means "little strings" in Italian. These long, thin strands of pasta are round and solid.

Tortelli: A round type of ravioli whose name literally means "little torte." Usually cut in a shape resembling a shiny sun, it can also have a half-moon shape. This pasta is usually served with light sauces so the flavor of the filling comes through.

Tortellini: Little rings of pasta filled with cheese, originally from the city of Bologna. Both plain and spinach-flavored tortellini are available; the fresh, refrigerated products are offered with a variety of fillings such as Italian sausage or chicken. Usually served with a tomato or cream sauce, tortellini is also well-suited to soups and salads. To prevent tortellini from losing its shape and filling, do not overcook it.

Vermicelli: A long, very thin pasta. "Little worms" is the original meaning of this word, which describes the squirming motion the noodles undergo when surrounded by sauce and twirled around a fork. It was the original pasta for spaghetti and meatballs. Vermicelli is well-suited for use with lighter sauces and in soups.

Wonton Wrappers: See Egg Roll Wrappers (page 7).

Ziti: A short cut, 2-inch tubular noodle with a smooth surface. It is well-suited for chunky sauces and meat sauces.

1. *Chinese Noodles*   2. *Fettuccine*   3. *Vermicelli*   4. *Somen*   5. *Linguine*   6. *Ziti*   7. *Egg Noodles* 8. *Tortellini*
9. *Wagon Wheels*   10. *Elbow Macaroni*   11. *Gemilli*   12. *Manicotti*   13. *Rotini*   14. *Farfalle (Bow Ties)*
15. *Radiatore (Nugget)*   16. *Fusilli*   17. *Ditali*   18. *Rigatoni*   19. *Gnocchi* 20. *Ravioli*   21. *Curly Noodles*

21

31

32

3

27

33

2

24

28

25

19

23

29

34

26

30

35

22. *Acini de Pepe* 23. *Penne* 24. *Medium Shells* 25. *Couscous* 26. *Medium Egg Noodles* 27. *Rotelle*
28. *Rosamarina (Orzo)* 29. *Small Shells* 30. *Heart-shaped Pasta* 31. *Jumbo Shells* 32. *Lasagna Noodles*
33. *Spaghetti* 34. *Rice Stick Noodles* 35. *Capellini (Angel Hair)*

SELECTION, STORAGE AND COOKING TIPS

SELECTION

Pasta is available in three forms: dried, fresh and frozen. Dried pasta is usually found prepackaged or in self-serve bulk form. Fresh pasta can be found in the refrigerated section of the supermarket. The most common varieties of frozen pasta are lasagna noodles, egg noodles and filled tortellini or ravioli.

- When purchasing dried pasta, look for smooth, unbroken pasta.

- Avoid dried pasta with a marblelike (many fine lines) surface; this indicates a problem with the way it dried and it may fall apart during cooking.

- When purchasing fresh pasta, look for smooth, unbroken pasta with consistent color throughout the shape. Although fresh pasta should appear dry, it shouldn't appear brittle or crumbly. Avoid packages containing moisture droplets or liquid, which could indicate molding or mushy pasta.

- When purchasing frozen pasta, avoid packages containing ice crystals or those in which the pasta pieces are frozen together in a solid mass. Avoid pasta that is freezer burned (dry, white spots).

STORAGE

Uncooked Dried Pasta: Most dried pasta can be stored indefinitely, but for optimum quality and flavor, a one- to two-year storage time is recommended.

- Store in original packaging or transfer to airtight glass or plastic containers and label contents with starting storage date.

- Store in a cool (60°F or less), dry location.

Uncooked Fresh Purchased Pasta: Fresh pasta is perishable and should be stored in the refrigerator. Most fresh pasta packages carry use-by or expiration dates.

- Store unopened pasta in original packaging.

- Cover opened, unused portions of pasta tightly to avoid drying.

Uncooked Frozen Pasta: Frozen pasta should be stored in the freezer until ready to cook.

- Store unopened pasta in original packaging.

- Store opened, unused portions tightly sealed to avoid freezer burn and drying.

- Freeze unopened pasta for up to 9 months.

- Freeze opened pasta for up to 3 months.

Cooked Dried, Fresh and Frozen Pasta: To prevent sticking, cooked pasta can be tossed with a small amount of oil before storing. Store in tightly sealed containers or plastic bags in the refrigerator for up to 5 days.

COOKING TIPS

Always cook pasta uncovered at a fast and continuous boil, using plenty of water. This allows the pasta to move freely, allowing it to cook evenly and prevent sticky pasta. Be sure the water is boiling vigorously before adding pasta.

- Do not add oil to the cooking water; it isn't necessary and sauces will not cling to oil-coated pasta.

- Salting the cooking water is optional and not necessary for the proper cooking of pasta.

- Use at least 1 quart water (4 cups) for every 4 ounces of pasta.

- Follow package directions for cooking times or refer to our **Pasta Cook Time Chart** on page 14. Fresh pasta cooks faster than dried pasta. Cooked pasta should be tender but firm to the bite (*al dente*).

- Stir pasta frequently to prevent sticking.

- Do not rinse pasta after draining unless stated in the recipe. Pasta is usually rinsed when it is to be used in cold salads.

REHEATING PASTA

Leftover pasta can save precious time during the middle of the week when every minute counts to get dinner on the table.

To reheat pasta, choose one of the three simple methods below:

1. Place pasta in rapidly boiling water for up to 2 minutes. Drain and serve immediately.

2. Place pasta in a colander and pour boiling water over it until heated through. Drain and serve immediately.

3. Place pasta in a microwave-safe dish or container. Microwave tightly covered on high for 1 to 3 minutes or until heated through. Serve immediately.

CHOOSING FLOUR FOR MAKING PASTA

Wheat, which is ground into flour, is what gives pasta its structure and texture. Basically, there are three types of flour to use to make homemade pasta.

1. Semolina Flour—Semolina flour is made from durum wheat. Durum wheat is a variety of wheat particularly high in gluten, the substance that gives bread dough its elasticity. Although high in gluten, durum wheat doesn't produce satisfactory baked goods, but it makes excellent pasta. The dry pasta you buy at the store is made with durum wheat. Semolina flour is more coarsely ground than most flour and looks similar to yellow cornmeal, but is paler in color and more finely ground. Semolina flour may be difficult to find, but is likely to be available in most large supermarkets, gourmet shops, Italian markets or through mail-order sources. Pasta dough made with semolina is slightly drier and stiffer than dough made with other flours because it absorbs liquid more easily.

2. All-purpose Flour—All-purpose flour, as its name implies, can be used for making all types of baked goods and is excellent for making pasta too. This flour is a blend of hard and soft wheat varieties, not durum wheat. Because of the type of wheat used in all-purpose flour, pasta dough is easy to work with and handle. You will notice how smooth and elastic the dough is when made with all-purpose flour.

3. Unbleached Flour—Unbleached flour is more cream colored than all-purpose flour (most all-purpose flour is made more white by a bleaching process) and has a slightly higher protein content. Unbleached flour will yield the same results as all-purpose flour.

> **NOTE:** All three flours are interchangeable in scratch pasta recipes, so if a recipe calls for 1 cup all-purpose flour, you could substitute 1 cup of semolina or unbleached flour.

PASTA COOK TIME CHART

Although most pasta packages have cooking directions, many people repackage their pasta into other containers and so have no directions. This handy reference chart gives cooking directions for the most popular types of pasta.

Dry Pasta Type	Cooking Time in Minutes
Acini de Pepe	5 to 6
Capellini (angel hair)	5 to 6
Egg Noodles (regular and wide)	8 to 10 regular; 10 to 12 extra wide
Elbow Macaroni	8 to 10
Farfalle (bow ties)	3 to 15
Fettuccine	11 to 13
Fusilli	11 to 13
Japanese Curly Noodles	4 to 5
Jumbo Shells	12 to 15
Lasagna Noodles	12 to 15
Linguine	9 to 13
Mafalde (mini-lasagna noodles)	8 to 10
Manicotti	10 to 12
Medium Shells	9 to 11
Mostaccioli	12 to 14
Penne	9 to 13
Radiatore (nugget)	9 to 11
Rigatoni	9 to 11
Rosamarina (orzo)	8 to 10
Rotelle	10 to 12
Rotini	8 to 10
Small Shells	9 to 11
Soba (buckwheat)	6 to 7
Spaghetti	8 to 10
Vermicelli	5 to 7
Wagon Wheel	10 to 12
Ziti	14 to 15

Fresh Pasta Type (purchased)	Cooking Time in Minutes
Capellini (angel hair)	1 to 2
Farfalle (bow ties)	2 to 3
Fettuccine	1 to 2
Lasagna	2 to 3
Linguine	1 to 2
Ravioli	6 to 8
Tortellini	8 to 10

HOW TO SUBSTITUTE PASTA SHAPES

With so many types of pasta shapes available, you may not have the shape called for in a recipe but yet you still would like to make that particular recipe. Can you substitute one pasta shape for another?

The answer is yes and the solution is easy. Pasta shapes can be substituted for one another as long as they are similar in size. The chart below gives a few examples to give you the idea of correct substitutions to make.

Type of Pasta	Substitution
Fettuccine	Linguine
Spaghetti	Vermicelli or Capellini (angel hair)
Rosamarina (orzo)	Acini de pepe
Rotini	Rotelle or radiatore
Penne	Mostaccioli or ziti
Farfalle (bow ties)	Rotini or rotelle
Wagon Wheel	Radiatore, rotini or rotelle

MATCHING PASTA AND SAUCES

The perfect pairing of pasta and sauce can greatly enhance both the flavor of the dish as well as the ease of eating the dish. Some shapes can be used in several different ways. Use the simple guidelines below for the perfect match.

Flat, Narrow and Thin Shapes (capellini, fettuccine, linguine, spaghetti, vermicelli): Smoother, thinner sauces or those with very finely chopped ingredients are the best choice because they will cling better to the large surface area of these pastas. Examples include: Alfredo Sauce (page 132) and Basil Pesto (page 142).

Short, Wide and Sturdy Shapes (mostaccioli, penne, rotelle, rotini, ziti): Chunky or heavy sauces are the best choice because the pasta is sturdy enough to hold up to these ingredients. Examples include: Bolognese Sauce (page 144) and Tomato Cream Sauce (page 143).

Hollow Shapes, Twist Shapes and Shapes with Crevices (radiatore, rigatoni, rotelle, rotini, shells): Sauces with small pieces of meat and vegetables are a good choice because the pasta can capture these bits in their crevices and hollow areas. Examples include: Turkey Taco Shells (page 88) and Chicken with Apricot Cream Sauce (page 102).

These pasta shapes also hold up well with chunky and heavy sauces (see **Short, Wide and Sturdy Shapes**).

1

PASTA FROM SCRATCH

Fresh Pasta: Cornmeal Pasta (p. 20),
Broccoli Pasta (p. 20), Spinach Pasta (p. 19),
Roasted Red Bell Pepper Pasta (p. 21)

FRESH PASTA

8 SERVINGS

5 large eggs

1 teaspoon olive or vegetable oil

1/4 teaspoon salt

3 cups all-purpose flour

Prepare as directed below for Hand Mixing or Food Processor Mixing. Roll, cut and cook as directed on pages 22–23.

Hand Mixing: Beat eggs, oil and salt in large bowl with wire whisk until smooth. Add flour. Mix thoroughly with fork until dough forms. (If dough is too dry, mix in enough water to make dough easy to handle. If dough is too sticky, gradually add flour when kneading.) Knead on lightly floured surface 5 to 10 minutes or until smooth and elastic. Cover with plastic wrap or aluminum foil. Let stand 15 minutes.

Food Processor Mixing: Place eggs, oil and salt in food processor. Cover and process until smooth. Add flour. Cover and process about 10 seconds or until dough leaves side of bowl and can be pressed together with fingers. (If dough is too dry, add a few drops of water; cover and process 5 seconds. If dough is too sticky, add a small amount of flour; cover and process 5 seconds.) Remove dough and press into a ball. Cover dough with plastic wrap or aluminum foil. Let stand 10 minutes.

1 Serving: Calories 210 (Calories from Fat 35); Fat 4g (Saturated 1g); Cholesterol 135mg; Sodium 110mg; Carbohydrate 36g (Dietary Fiber 1g); Protein 8g.

PASTA YIELDS

- When preparing pasta, allow 1/2 to 3/4 cup cooked pasta per side dish or appetizer serving. If you plan to make pasta your main dish, allow 1 1/4 to 1 1/2 cups per serving.

- 2 ounces of dried pasta will yield approximately 1 to 1 1/2 cups of cooked pasta. The yield will vary slightly depending on the shape, type and size of pasta.

- To measure 4 ounces of spaghetti easily, make a circle with your thumb and index finger about the size of a quarter, then fill it with pasta!

Basic Pasta Yields

Uncooked	Cooked	Servings
Macaroni 6 or 7 ounces (2 cups)	4 cups	4 to 6
Spaghetti 7 to 8 ounces (2 cups)	4 cups	4 to 6
Noodles 8 ounces (4 to 5 cups)	4 to 5 cups	4 to 6

SPINACH PASTA

8 SERVINGS

8 ounces spinach*

2 large eggs

1 tablespoon olive or vegetable oil

1 teaspoon salt

2 cups all-purpose flour

Wash spinach; drain. Cover and cook in 2-quart saucepan over medium heat with just the water that clings to the leaves 3 to 10 minutes or until pasta is soft and limp. Rinse spinach in cold water; drain. Press spinach against side of strainer with back of spoon to remove excess water.

Place spinach, eggs, oil and salt in food processor or blender. Cover and process until smooth.

Continue as directed below for Hand Mixing or Food Processor Mixing. Roll, cut and cook as directed on pages 22–23.

Hand Mixing: Place spinach mixture in large bowl. Add flour. Mix thoroughly with fork until dough forms. (If dough is too dry, mix in enough water to make dough easy to handle. If dough is too sticky, gradually add flour when kneading.) Knead on lightly floured surface 5 to 10 minutes or until smooth and elastic. Cover with plastic wrap or aluminum foil. Let stand 15 minutes.

Food Processor Mixing: Add flour to spinach mixture in food processor. Cover and process about 10 seconds or until dough leaves side of bowl and can be pressed together with fingers. (If dough is too dry, add a few drops of water; cover and process 5 seconds. If dough is too sticky, add a small amount of flour; cover and process 5 seconds.) Remove dough and press into a ball. Cover dough with plastic wrap or aluminum foil. Let stand 10 minutes.

*1 package (10 ounces) frozen chopped spinach can be substituted for the fresh spinach. Cook as directed on package; squeeze to drain.

1 Serving: Calories 145 (Calories from Fat 25); Fat 3g (Saturated 1g); Cholesterol 55mg; Sodium 300mg; Carbohydrate 25g (Dietary Fiber 1g); Protein 5g.

USING OIL TO BOIL PASTA

Adding oil to the cooking water isn't necessary and doesn't prevent it from sticking. So how do you prevent pasta from sticking? A few simple methods will do the trick!

1. In a large saucepan, kettle, stockpot or Dutch oven, bring 4 to 6 quarts of water to boiling for 1 pound of pasta. For smaller amounts, the rule of thumb is to use 1 quart (4 cups) of water for every 4 ounces of pasta.

2. Add pasta gradually and allow the water to return to a boil. Keep the water boiling continuously during cooking; it needs room to "swim" to cook properly.

3. Stir the pasta right away and several times after the water returns to a boil. For long-shaped pasta (spaghetti, linguine, fettuccine, etc.) a long-handled fork works best for stirring. For short or small-shaped pasta (rotini, rigatoni, elbow macaroni) a wide spoon works best for stirring. Stirring pasta while it cooks prevents it from sticking together.

4. Drain and serve immediately. Pasta that will be used right away should not be rinsed unless the recipe specifically states to rinse. For storing pasta that won't be used immediately, toss with a small amount of oil to help prevent sticking. See Pasta Storage (page 12).

CORNMEAL PASTA

8 SERVINGS

1/2 cup canned whole kernel corn, well drained, or frozen whole kernel corn, thawed and drained

2 large eggs

1 tablespoon corn, olive or vegetable oil

1 teaspoon salt

2 cups all-purpose flour

1/2 cup yellow cornmeal

Place corn, eggs, oil and salt in food processor or blender. Cover and process until smooth.

Continue as directed below for Hand Mixing or Food Processor Mixing. Roll, cut and cook as directed on pages 22–23.

Hand Mixing: Place corn mixture in large bowl. Add flour and cornmeal. Mix thoroughly with fork until dough forms. (If dough is too dry, mix in enough water to make dough easy to handle. If dough is too sticky, gradually add flour when kneading.) Knead on lightly floured surface 5 to 10 minutes or until smooth and elastic. Cover with plastic wrap or aluminum foil. Let stand 15 minutes.

Food Processor Mixing: Add flour and cornmeal to corn mixture in food processor. Cover and process about 10 seconds or until dough leaves side of bowl and can be pressed together with fingers. (If dough is too dry, add a few drops of water; cover and process 5 seconds. If dough is too sticky, add a small amount of flour; cover and process 5 seconds.) Remove dough and press into a ball. Cover dough with plastic wrap or aluminum foil. Let stand 10 minutes.

1 Serving: Calories 190 (Calories from Fat 35); Fat 4g (Saturated 1g); Cholesterol 55mg; Sodium 320mg; Carbohydrate 33g (Dietary Fiber 1g); Protein 6g.

BROCCOLI PASTA

8 SERVINGS

1 1/2 cups chopped cooked broccoli, well drained

2 large eggs

1 tablespoon olive or vegetable oil

1 teaspoon salt

2 3/4 cups all-purpose flour

Place broccoli, eggs, oil and salt in food processor or blender. Cover and process until smooth.

Continue as directed below for Hand Mixing or Food Processor Mixing. Roll, cut and cook as directed on pages 22–23.

Hand Mixing: Place broccoli mixture in large bowl. Add flour. Mix thoroughly with fork until dough forms. (If dough is too dry, mix in enough water to make dough easy to handle. If dough is too sticky, gradually add flour when kneading.) Knead on lightly floured surface 5 to 10 minutes or until smooth and elastic. Cover with plastic wrap or aluminum foil. Let stand 15 minutes.

Food Processor Mixing: Add 2 cups of the flour to broccoli mixture in food processor. Cover and process until dough is well blended. Add remaining 3/4 cup flour. Cover and process about 10 seconds or until dough leaves side of bowl and can be pressed together with fingers. (If dough is too dry, add a few drops of water; cover and process 5 seconds. If dough is too sticky, add a small amount of flour; cover and process 5 seconds.) Remove dough and press into a ball. Cover dough with plastic wrap or aluminum foil. Let stand 10 minutes.

1 Serving: Calories 185 (Calories from Fat 25); Fat 3g (Saturated 1g); Cholesterol 55mg; Sodium 290mg; Carbohydrate 35g (Dietary Fiber 2g); Protein 7g.

ROASTED RED BELL PEPPER PASTA

8 SERVINGS

1 jar (12 ounces) roasted red bell peppers, well drained

1 tablespoon chopped oil-packed sun-dried tomatoes or sun-dried tomato paste

2 large eggs

1 tablespoon olive or vegetable oil

1 teaspoon salt

2 3/4 cups all-purpose flour

Place bell peppers and tomatoes in food processor or blender. Cover and process until smooth. Place mixture in strainer; press mixture against side of strainer with back of spoon to remove excess liquid.

Continue as directed below for Hand Mixing or Food Processor Mixing. Roll, cut and cook as directed on pages 22–23.

Hand Mixing: Beat pepper mixture, eggs, oil and salt in large bowl with wire whisk until smooth. Add flour. Mix thoroughly with fork until dough forms. (If dough is too dry, mix in enough water to make dough easy to handle. If dough is too sticky, gradually add flour when kneading.) Knead on lightly floured surface 5 to 10 minutes or until smooth and elastic. Cover with plastic wrap or aluminum foil. Let stand 15 minutes.

Food Processor Mixing: Place pepper mixture, eggs, oil and salt in food processor. Cover and process until smooth. Add 2 cups of the flour. Cover and process until dough is well blended. Add remaining 3/4 cup flour. Cover and process about 10 seconds or until dough leaves side of bowl and can be pressed together with fingers. (If dough is too dry, add a few drops of water; cover and process 5 seconds. If dough is too sticky, add a small amount of flour; cover and process 5 seconds.) Remove dough and press into a ball. Cover dough with plastic wrap or aluminum foil. Let stand 10 minutes.

1 Serving: Calories 195 (Calories from Fat 35); Fat 4g (Saturated 1g); Cholesterol 55mg; Sodium 290mg; Carbohydrate 36g (Dietary Fiber 2g); Protein 6g.

EASY HERB-FLAVORED PASTA

Looking for a quick way to jazz up the flavor of cooked pasta? Try adding 1 tablespoon of crushed dried herbs to the cooking water for 1 pound of pasta. Crushing the herbs before adding them to the water helps to release extra flavor. Try one of the combinations below for a quick and easy flavor boost.

Italian: Add crushed Italian seasoning, basil or oregano to cooking water. Toss pasta with olive oil or melted butter, Parmesan cheese and freshly ground pepper.

French: Add crushed tarragon to cooking water. Toss pasta with melted butter, whipping cream and cooked chicken.

Mexican: Add crushed oregano to cooking water. Toss pasta with salsa and black beans; sprinkle with Cheddar cheese.

Rolling, Cutting, Cooking and Storing Fresh Pasta

Hand Rolling:

Divide dough in half. Roll one-half of dough with rolling pin into rectangle 1/8 to 1/16 inch thick on lightly floured surface (keep remaining dough covered). Sprinkle dough lightly with flour. Loosely fold rectangle lengthwise into thirds; cut crosswise into 1/4-inch strips for fettuccine, 1/8-inch strips for linguine. Shake out strips. Hang pasta on pasta drying rack or arrange in single layer on lightly floured towels; sprinkle lightly with flour. Repeat with remaining dough. If pasta will not be cooked immediately, follow the **Storing** information below.

Manual Pasta Machine:

Divide dough in quarters. Flatten each quarter of dough with hands to 1/2-inch thickness on lightly floured surface (keep remaining dough covered). Feed one part dough through smooth rollers set at widest setting. Sprinkle with all-purpose flour if dough becomes sticky. Fold lengthwise into thirds. Repeat feeding dough through rollers and folding into thirds 8 to 10 times or until firm and smooth. Feed dough through progressively narrower settings (usually numbered 1 through 5 on most machines) until dough is 1/8 to 1/16 inch thick. (Dough will lengthen as it becomes thinner; it may be cut crosswise at any time for easier handling.) Feed dough through cutting rollers of desired shape. Shake out strips. Hang pasta on pasta drying rack or arrange in single layer on lightly floured towels; sprinkle lightly with flour. Repeat with remaining dough. If pasta will not be cooked immediately, follow the **Storing** information below.

Electric Extrusion Pasta Machines:

The scratch pasta recipes in this book were not developed for or tested in electric extrusion pasta machines. These machines generally have specific measuring devices for flour and liquid ingredients and specific directions unique to each machine. We recommend following manufacturer's directions for recipes, cutting and cooking fresh pasta if using an electric extrusion machine.

COOKING:

Heat 4 quarts water to boiling in 6- to 8-quart saucepan; add noodles. Boil uncovered 2 to 5 minutes, stirring occasionally, until firm but tender. Begin testing for doneness when noodles rise to surface of water. Drain noodles. Do not rinse.

STORING:

- **Refrigerator:** Toss fresh pasta lightly with flour. Allow to stand until partially dry but still pliable; loosely coil pasta into rounds for easier storage. Store in sealed plastic container or plastic bags for up to 3 days.

- **Freezer:** Toss fresh pasta lightly with flour. Allow to stand until partially dry but still pliable; loosely coil pasta into rounds for easier storage. Store in sealed plastic container or plastic bags for up to 1 month.

HANDLING FRESH PASTA:

Pasta that is completely dry is very fragile; handle carefully to avoid breakage.

FLAVORED PASTA:

By adding vegetables, herbs, spices and other ingredients to fresh pasta dough, you can achieve mild flavor and color. Keep in mind that the color will fade slightly upon cooking and the flavors are subtle and mild; not strong.

MUSHROOM-LEEK PASTA

8 SERVINGS

1 package (1 ounce) dried porcini or shiitake mushrooms (about 1 cup)

1/2 cup sliced leeks or green onions

5 large eggs

1 tablespoon olive or vegetable oil

1/4 teaspoon salt

3 1/2 cups all-purpose flour

Place dried mushrooms (do not rehydrate) and leeks in food processor or blender. Cover and process, stopping occasionally to scrape sides, until coarsely chopped. Add eggs, oil and salt. Cover and process until mushrooms are finely chopped.

Continue as directed below for Hand Mixing or Food Processor Mixing. Roll, cut and cook as directed on pages 22–23.

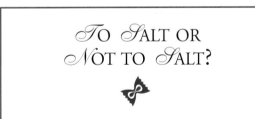 **Hand Mixing:** Place mushroom mixture in large bowl. Add flour. Mix thoroughly with fork until dough forms. (If dough is too dry, mix in enough water to make dough easy to handle. If dough is too sticky, gradually add flour when kneading.) Knead on lightly floured surface 5 to 10 minutes or until smooth and elastic. Cover with plastic wrap or aluminum foil. Let stand 15 minutes.

Food Processor Mixing: Add 3 cups of the flour to mushroom mixture in food processor. Cover and process until dough is well blended. Add remaining 1/2 cup flour. Cover and process about 10 seconds or until dough leaves side of bowl and can be pressed together with fingers. (If dough is too dry, add a few drops of water; cover and process 5 seconds. If dough is too sticky, add a small amount of flour; cover and process 5 seconds.) Remove dough and press into a ball. Cover dough with plastic wrap or aluminum foil. Let stand 10 minutes.

1 Serving: Calories 250 (Calories from Fat 45); Fat 5g (Saturated 1g); Cholesterol 135mg; Sodium 110mg; Carbohydrate 43g (Dietary Fiber 2g); Protein 10g.

TO SALT OR NOT TO SALT?

Salt isn't necessary for the proper cooking of pasta; it simply adds flavor and adding it is a matter of personal preference. If you are watching your salt intake, but would like to add extra flavor to your pasta, try adding 1 to 2 tablespoons of lemon or lime juice to the cooking water.

Note: The nutrition calculations for the recipes in this book do not include the use of salt in the cooking water.

CHEESE-PEPPER PASTA

8 SERVINGS

5 large eggs
1/4 cup grated Parmesan cheese
1/4 cup grated Romano cheese
1 tablespoon olive or vegetable oil
1 teaspoon coarsely ground pepper
3 cups all-purpose flour

Prepare as directed below for Hand Mixing or Food Processor Mixing. Roll, cut and cook as directed on pages 22–23.

Hand Mixing: Beat eggs, cheeses, oil and pepper in large bowl with wire whisk until smooth. Add flour. Mix thoroughly with fork until dough forms. (If dough is too dry, mix in enough water to make dough easy to handle. If dough is too sticky, gradually add flour when kneading.) Knead on lightly floured surface 5 to 10 minutes or until smooth and elastic. Cover with plastic wrap or aluminum foil. Let stand 15 minutes.

Food Processor Mixing: Place eggs, cheeses, oil and pepper in food processor. Cover and process until smooth. Add flour. Cover and process about 10 seconds or until dough leaves side of bowl and can be pressed together with fingers. (If dough is too dry, add a few drops of water; cover and process 5 seconds. If dough is too sticky, add a small amount of flour; cover and process 5 seconds.) Remove dough and press into a ball. Cover dough with plastic wrap or aluminum foil. Let stand 10 minutes.

1 Serving: Calories 250 (Calories from Fat 65); Fat 7g (Saturated 2g); Cholesterol 135mg; Sodium 130mg; Carbohydrate 37g (Dietary Fiber 1g); Protein 11g.

ROSEMARY-LEMON PASTA

8 SERVINGS

5 large eggs
2 tablespoons chopped fresh or 2 teaspoons dried rosemary leaves
1 tablespoon plus 1 teaspoon grated lemon peel
1 tablespoon olive or vegetable oil
1/4 teaspoon salt
3 1/4 cups all-purpose flour

Prepare as directed below for Hand Mixing or Food Processor Mixing. Roll, cut and cook as directed on pages 22–23.

Hand Mixing: Beat eggs, rosemary, lemon peel, oil and salt in large bowl with wire whisk until smooth. Add flour. Mix thoroughly with fork until dough forms. (If dough is too dry, mix in enough water to make dough easy to handle. If dough is too sticky, gradually add flour when kneading.) Knead on lightly floured surface 5 to 10 minutes or until smooth and elastic. Cover with plastic wrap or aluminum foil. Let stand 15 minutes.

Food Processor Mixing: Place eggs, rosemary, lemon peel, oil and salt in food processor. Cover and process until smooth. Add flour. Cover and process about 10 seconds or until dough leaves side of bowl and can be pressed together with fingers. (If dough is too dry, add a few drops of water; cover and process 5 seconds. If dough is too sticky, add a small amount of flour; cover and process 5 seconds.) Remove dough and press into a ball. Cover dough with plastic wrap or aluminum foil. Let stand 10 minutes.

1 Serving: Calories 230 (Calories from Fat 45); Fat 5g (Saturated 1g); Cholesterol 135mg; Sodium 110mg; Carbohydrate 39g (Dietary Fiber 2g); Protein 9g.

Rosemary-Lemon Pasta

2

APPETIZERS

Crispy Chili Twists (p. 30),
Marinated Balsamic Pasta and
Vegetables (p. 44)

CRISPY CHILI TWISTS

16 APPETIZER SERVINGS

Here's a spicy alternative to chips using pasta as a base. They also add some crunch and zip to a soup or sandwich meal.

2 cups uncooked rotini pasta (6 ounces)
Vegetable oil
2 tablespoons grated Parmesan cheese
1/2 teaspoon chili powder
1/4 teaspoon seasoned salt
1/8 teaspoon garlic powder

Cook and drain pasta as directed on package. Rinse with cold water; drain very thoroughly (excess water on pasta will cause oil to spatter).

Heat oil (1 inch) to 375°. Fry pasta, about 1 cup at a time, about 2 minutes or until crisp and light golden brown, stirring if necessary to separate. Drain on paper towels. Mix remaining ingredients in large bowl; toss with pasta until evenly coated.

1 Serving (1/4 cup): Calories 80 (Calories from Fat 20); Fat 2g (Saturated 0g); Cholesterol 0mg; Sodium 35mg; Carbohydrate 13g (Dietary Fiber 0g); Protein 2g.

BAKED RAVIOLI

12 SERVINGS

2 packages (9 ounces each) refrigerated filled ravioli (any flavor)
1/4 cup margarine, butter or spread, melted
1/2 cup Italian-style dry bread crumbs
1/4 cup finely shredded Parmesan cheese
1/8 teaspoon coarsely ground pepper
2 tablespoons chopped fresh parsley

Heat oven to 400°. Grease rectangular baking dish, 11 × 7 × 1 1/2 inches. Cook and drain ravioli as directed on package.

Toss ravioli and margarine in baking dish. Mix remaining ingredients, except parsley. Toss ravioli and bread crumb mixture; spread evenly in dish. Sprinkle with parsley. Bake uncovered about 15 to 20 minutes or until mixture is hot and topping is golden brown.

1 Serving: Calories 110 (Calories from Fat 55); Fat 6g (Saturated 2g); Cholesterol 5mg; Sodium 340mg; Carbohydrate 11g (Dietary Fiber 0g); Protein 3g.

CREAMY ARUGULA PASTA WITH CHÈVRE

4 SERVINGS

For an attractive garnish, cut 1/4-inch slices of goat cheese into fun and attractive shapes with canapé cutters or a knife. Place shapes on top of each serving of pasta, and sprinkle with bell pepper.

1/2 cup sour cream

1/4 teaspoon salt

1/8 teaspoon pepper

1/2 cup milk

4 ounces chèvre (goat) cheese

2 bunches arugula (about 6 ounces)

8 ounces uncooked capellini (angel hair) pasta

1/4 cup finely chopped red bell pepper

Heat sour cream, salt, pepper, milk and cheese in 1-quart saucepan over low heat, stirring frequently, until cheese is melted and mixture is smooth; remove from heat.

Heat 4 quarts water to boiling in Dutch oven. Place arugula in wire mesh strainer. Plunge strainer into water about 20 seconds or just until arugula is wilted; drain (do not discard water).

Cook and drain pasta as directed on package, using water in Dutch oven. In medium bowl, toss together pasta, arugula and cheese mixture. Sprinkle with bell pepper.

1 Serving: Calories 375 (Calories from Fat 115); Fat 13g (Saturated 8g); Cholesterol 45mg; Sodium 270mg; Carbohydrate 50g (Dietary Fiber 2g); Protein 14g.

SWEET CHEESE PANZOTTI

8 SERVINGS

"Pot-bellied" panzotti are triangular or round dumplings usually filled with a spinach-cheese mixture. We've filled ours with a refreshing combination of ricotta, honey and spices and added a savory, buttery sauce.

8 wonton wrappers

1 cup ricotta cheese

1/2 cup golden raisins

1 tablespoon honey

3/4 teaspoon ground cinnamon

1/8 teaspoon ground nutmeg

3 tablespoons margarine, butter or spread

1 tablespoon chopped fresh or 1 teaspoon dried sage leaves

1/8 teaspoon coarsely ground pepper

Mix cheese, raisins, honey, cinnamon and nutmeg. Spoon about 1 tablespoon ricotta mixture onto center of each wonton. Moisten edges of wrappers lightly with water. Fold diagonally in half over filling, forming a triangle; press gently around filling to seal.

Heat 2 tablespoons of the margarine, the sage and pepper in 10-inch skillet over medium heat until margarine is melted. Add half of the panzotti. Cook about 5 minutes, turning occasionally, until tender. Remove panzotti from skillet; keep warm.

Melt remaining 1 tablespoon margarine in skillet. Add remaining panzotti. Cook about 5 minutes, turning occasionally, until tender. Drizzle panzotti with any remaining margarine mixture.

1 Serving: Calories 165 (Calories from Fat 65); Fat 7g (Saturated 3g); Cholesterol 10mg; Sodium 230mg; Carbohydrate 22g (Dietary Fiber 1g); Protein 5g.

Sweet Cheese Panzotti

Dessert "Pastabilities"

"Life is uncertain, so eat dessert first!" To many, dessert is an absolute must. It's a reward, a special treat to be savored. Whether it's a simple piece of fruit, flavored coffee, cake, pie, cookies or ice cream, the self-proclaimed dessert lover is always looking to satisfy his or her sweet tooth.

Although pasta doesn't generally come to mind as a dessert, consider that pasta has been a key ingredient for decades in the traditional Jewish specialty known as kugel or noodle pudding. And, in many cases, pasta is used as rice is in desserts similar to rice pudding.

The recipes we've developed will definitely satisfy your sweet tooth and surprise your taste buds. Our desserts capture favorite and familiar flavors such as cherry crisp, decadently topped cheesecake and creamy rice pudding. Not only are they fun to eat, but they taste terrific and are very easy to prepare!

Noodle Pudding

8 SERVINGS

There are many variations on this creamy noodle pudding, which is found in Jewish homes from Eastern Europe to Israel.

**4 cups uncooked wide egg noodles
(8 ounces)**

1 cup sour cream

1 cup small curd cottage cheese

1/2 cup raisins

1/2 cup sugar

1 teaspoon ground cinnamon

1/4 teaspoon ground nutmeg

2 eggs, slightly beaten

Heat oven to 350°. Grease 2-quart casserole. Cook and drain noodles as directed on package.

Mix noodles and remaining ingredients. Pour into casserole. Bake uncovered 40 to 50 minutes or until golden brown.

1 Serving: Calories 275 (Calories from Fat 80); Fat 9g (Saturated 5g); Cholesterol 100mg; Sodium 140mg; Carbohydrate 41g (Dietary Fiber 1g); Protein 9g.

CREAMY COUSCOUS-DATE PUDDING

4 SERVINGS

Couscous, the smallest form of pasta, is one of the quickest foods there is—here's a dessert version that couldn't be easier.

2 cups milk

1 package (4-serving size) vanilla
   pudding and pie filling
   (not instant)

1/4 cup uncooked couscous

1/4 cup chopped dates or raisins

1/4 cup slivered almonds, toasted

Mix milk and pudding and pie filling (dry) in 2-quart saucepan until blended. Stir in couscous and dates.

Heat to boiling over medium heat, stirring frequently; remove from heat. Cover and let stand 5 minutes. Stir in almonds.

1 Serving: Calories 270 (Calories from Fat 65); Fat 7g (Saturated 2g); Cholesterol 10mg; Sodium 220mg; Carbohydrate 47g (Dietary Fiber 2g); Protein 7g.

(Continued on next page)

CHERRY-STREUSEL LASAGNA

6 SERVINGS

If you like cherry crisp or cherry crumble, you'll love this sweet treat!

4 uncooked lasagna noodles

Streusel (below)

2 packages (8 ounces each) cream
cheese, softened

1/2 cup sugar

1/2 cup milk

1/2 teaspoon almond extract

2 eggs

1 can (21 ounces) cherry pie filling

Heat oven to 325°. Grease rectangular baking dish, 11×7×1 1/2 inches. Cook and drain noodles as directed on package. Prepare Streusel; set aside.

Beat cream cheese and sugar in medium bowl with electric mixer on medium speed about 30 seconds or until fluffy. Beat in milk, almond extract and eggs on low speed about 30 seconds or until smooth.

Spread about 1/2 cup of the pie filling in baking dish. Top with 2 noodles. Pour half of the cream cheese mixture (about 1 1/2 cups) over noodles. Spread half of the remaining pie filling (about 3/4 cup) over cream cheese mixture. Repeat layers, starting with remaining 2 noodles. Sprinkle with Streusel.

Bake 50 to 55 minutes or until knife inserted in center comes out clean. Let stand 15 minutes. Serve warm or cool. Cover and refrigerate any remaining dessert.

STREUSEL

1/4 cup quick-cooking or
old-fashioned oats

1/4 cup packed brown sugar

1/4 cup chopped pecans

3 tablespoons margarine, butter or
spread, softened

1 tablespoon all-purpose flour

Mix all ingredients until crumbly.

1 Serving: Calories 645 (Calories from Fat 340); Fat 38g (Saturated 19g); Cholesterol 155mg; Sodium 330mg; Carbohydrate 67g (Dietary Fiber 2g); Protein 11g

Chocolate Chip-Pecan Shells with Caramel Sauce

8 SERVINGS

The rich filling in these shells tastes like cheesecake. Photo on p. 38.

16 uncooked jumbo pasta shells

1 1/4 cups ricotta cheese

1/2 cup powdered sugar

1 1/2 teaspoons vanilla

1 1/2 cups frozen (thawed) whipped topping

1/4 cup miniature semisweet chocolate chips

1/4 cup chopped pecans, toasted if desired

1 cup chocolate or caramel ice-cream topping, warmed

Cook and drain pasta as directed on package; pat dry. Beat cheese, powdered sugar and vanilla in medium bowl with electric mixer on medium speed about 3 minutes or until light and creamy. Fold in whipped topping. Fold in chocolate chips and pecans.

Spoon about 2 1/2 tablespoons cheese mixture into each pasta shell. Place in shallow container. Cover with plastic wrap and refrigerate at least 2 hours but no longer than 8 hours. Serve with ice-cream topping, and if desired, sprinkle with additional chocolate chips and pecans.

1 Serving: Calories 350 (Calories from Fat 100); Fat 11g (Saturated 6g); Cholesterol 10mg; Sodium 200mg; Carbohydrate 56g (Dietary Fiber 1g); Protein 8g.

BROCCOLI AND GARLIC FUSILLI

8 SERVINGS

1 1/2 cups uncooked tricolor fusilli pasta (4 ounces)

2 cups small broccoli flowerets

1/4 cup olive or vegetable oil

2 cloves garlic, finely chopped

1/4 cup margarine, butter or spread

1/2 teaspoon anchovy paste

1/4 cup shredded Parmesan cheese

2 tablespoons pine nuts or slivered almonds

Cook pasta as directed on package, adding broccoli 3 minutes before pasta is done; drain.

Heat oil in 10-inch skillet over medium heat. Cook garlic in oil about 1 minute, stirring occasionally, until golden. Stir in margarine and anchovy paste until margarine is melted.

Add pasta and broccoli; toss until heated through. Toss with cheese and pine nuts.

1 Serving: Calories 220 (Calories from Fat 135); Fat 15g (Saturated 3g); Cholesterol 25mg; Sodium 130mg; Carbohydrate 18g (Dietary Fiber 2g); Protein 5g.

PEAR AND PROSCIUTTO PASTA

8 SERVINGS

2 cups uncooked farfalle (bow tie) pasta (4 ounces)

2 medium pears, peeled if desired, and coarsely chopped (2 cups)

2 tablespoons lemon juice

1/4 cup margarine, butter or spread

1/2 cup diced prosciutto

2 tablespoons packed brown sugar

1/4 teaspoon coarsely ground pepper

Cook and drain pasta as directed on package; keep warm. Toss pears with lemon juice to prevent browning; drain.

Melt margarine in 10-inch skillet over medium heat. Stir in prosciutto, brown sugar and pepper until sugar is melted. Cook pears in brown sugar mixture, stirring occasionally, until tender. Toss with pasta.

1 Serving: Calories 155 (Calories from Fat 65); Fat 7g (Saturated 2g); Cholesterol 5mg; Sodium 150mg; Carbohydrate 21g (Dietary Fiber 2g); Protein 4g.

Chocolate Chip-Pecan Shells with Caramel Sauce (page 37)

TANGY BACON-TOPPED TORTELLINI

ABOUT 38 APPETIZERS

1 package (9 ounces) refrigerated cheese-filled tortellini

1/2 cup pitted dates

1/2 cup dried apricots

1/2 cup pimiento-stuffed olives

1/4 cup orange juice

1/2 pound bacon, crisply cooked and crumbled (1 cup)

Heat oven to 375°. Grease rectangular baking dish, 13 × 9 × 2 inches. Cook and drain tortellini as directed on package. Arrange in single layer in baking dish.

Place dates, apricots, olives and orange juice in food processor or blender. Cover and process until finely chopped. Sprinkle over tortellini. Sprinkle with bacon.

Bake uncovered about 20 minutes or until hot. Serve warm with toothpicks.

1 Appetizer: Calories 35 (Calories from Fat 10); Fat 1g (Saturated 0g); Cholesterol 5mg; Sodium 100mg; Carbohydrate 5g (Dietary Fiber 0g); Protein 1g.

COMBINING FRESH HERBS

Fresh, aromatic herbs heighten the flavor of foods. The best way to learn about the flavor herbs impart is by experimenting and tasting the food. Start with a small amount of unfamiliar herbs or herb combinations and then taste the food—more herbs can be added until the desired flavor is reached.

Fresh herbs lose their flavor if cooked too long, so add them during the last 10 to 15 minutes of cooking. Add fresh herbs to cold food right away so the flavors have a chance to blend.

When combining herbs, it's best not to combine certain strong herbs because their individual flavors will compete and cancel each other out. However, sage and thyme or rosemary and thyme can be combined with delicious results, such as in traditional turkey stuffing. Strong herbs are best combined with the medium or mild flavored herbs listed in the chart below.

Strong Herbs	Medium Herbs	Mild Herbs
Cilantro	Basil	Chives
Oregano	Marjoram	Dill Weed
Rosemary	Mint	Parsley
Sage		
Tarragon		
Thyme		

TORTELLINI IN CREAMY SPINACH-THYME PESTO

6 SERVINGS

This delicious appetizer can also serve three as a main dish. Try sliced vine-ripened tomatoes for a pretty and flavorful accompaniment.

1 package (9 ounces) refrigerated filled tortellini or ravioli (any flavor)

1 container (10 ounces) Alfredo sauce

1 1/2 cups packed spinach leaves

1/4 cup chicken broth

3 tablespoons grated Parmesan cheese

2 teaspoons lightly packed fresh thyme leaves

1 teaspoon olive or vegetable oil

1/8 teaspoon pepper

1 clove garlic

Heat oven to 350°. Grease 1 1/2-quart casserole. Cook and drain tortellini as directed on package. Place tortellini in casserole; toss with Alfredo sauce.

Place remaining ingredients in food processor or blender. Cover and process until smooth. Toss spinach mixture and tortellini mixture.

Cover and bake about 20 minutes or until hot. Garnish with additional grated Parmesan cheese if desired.

1 Serving: Calories 335 (Calories from Fat 245); Fat 27g (Saturated 14g); Cholesterol 105mg; Sodium 460mg; Carbohydrate 14g (Dietary Fiber 1g); Protein 10g.

GNOCCHI DIABLO

8 SERVINGS

Diablo means "devil," and this appetizer is appropriately named, thanks to the fiery kick in its sauce.

1/2 package (24-ounce size) frozen gnocchi

1/2 pound bulk hot Italian sausage

1 medium onion, cut into thin wedges

2 cups spaghetti sauce

1/8 teaspoon crushed red pepper

1 tablespoon chopped fresh or 1 teaspoon dried basil leaves

1 tablespoon grated Parmesan cheese

Cook and drain gnocchi as directed on package; keep warm. Cook sausage and onion in 1 1/2-quart saucepan over medium-high heat, stirring occasionally, until sausage is no longer pink; drain. Stir in spaghetti sauce and red pepper. Heat to boiling; reduce heat to low. Cover and simmer 5 minutes.

Spoon sauce mixture onto serving plates. Top with gnocchi. Sprinkle with basil and cheese.

1 Serving: Calories 200 (Calories from Fat 90); Fat 10g (Saturated 3g); Cholesterol 25mg; Sodium 705mg; Carbohydrate 23g (Dietary Fiber 3g); Protein 8g.

CAESAR TORTELLINI

12 SERVINGS

Inspired by the popular salad, this appetizer is easy to prepare because there are no fussy pieces to assemble. Simply place the bowl out with some toothpicks nearby, and let your guests put together their own appetizers.

1 package (9 ounces) refrigerated filled tortellini (any flavor)

1/2 cup Caesar dressing

1/4 cup grated Parmesan cheese

12 ounces cherry tomatoes (about 21 tomatoes)

1 can (6 ounces) pitted large ripe olives, drained

Salad greens

Cook and drain tortellini as directed on package. Toss tortellini, dressing and cheese. Cover and refrigerate at least 4 hours but no longer than 24 hours, tossing occasionally.

Toss tortellini mixture and additional dressing if desired. Toss tortellini mixture, tomatoes and olives. Line large bowl with salad greens. Place tortellini mixture in bowl. Serve with toothpicks.

1 Serving: Calories 125 (Calories from Fat 80); Fat 9g (Saturated 2g); Cholesterol 20mg; Sodium 340mg; Carbohydrate 8g (Dietary Fiber 1g); Protein 4g.

PASTA TORTE SLICES

12 SERVINGS

For an impressive start to your next entertaining meal, here's a do-ahead recipe which combines some favorite pasta-loving ingredients into a visually stunning result. A few fresh basil leaves is all you'll need for garnish.

6 uncooked lasagna noodles

1 package (8 ounces) cream cheese, softened

2 tablespoons chopped oil-packed sun-dried tomatoes

1 container (7 ounces) pesto

1/2 cup margarine, butter or spread, softened

1 package (10 ounces) frozen chopped broccoli, cooked, drained and cooled

1 jar (30 ounces) spaghetti sauce (about 3 cups)

1/4 cup pine nuts, toasted

Cook and drain noodles as directed on package. Mix cream cheese and tomatoes. Mix pesto and margarine in medium bowl. Stir in broccoli. Spread about 3 tablespoons cream cheese mixture evenly over each lasagna noodle; spread about 1/3 cup broccoli mixture evenly over cream cheese mixture. Roll up noodles. Place seam-side-down in shallow container. Cover and refrigerate at least 4 hours but no longer than 24 hours or until firm. To serve, cut each roll in half, forming two rounds.

Heat spaghetti sauce until hot in 1 1/2-quart saucepan. Place about 1/4 cup sauce onto individual serving plates. Arrange 1 slice on sauce on each plate. Sprinkle with pine nuts.

1 Serving: Calories 330 (Calories from Fat 245); Fat 27g (Saturated 8g); Cholesterol 25mg; Sodium 687mg; Carbohydrate 18g (Dietary Fiber 2g); Protein 6g.

Marinated Balsamic Pasta and Vegetables

18 APPETIZERS

Peel the pearl onions quickly and easily by dropping them into the boiling water before cooking the pasta. After a few minutes, remove the onions from the water, and the skins will slip right off.

2 1/2 cups uncooked radiatore (nugget) pasta (8 ounces)

18 pearl onions

6 ounces whole green beans

1 large red bell pepper, cut into 1-inch pieces

1 large yellow bell pepper, cut into 1-inch pieces

1/2 cup sugar

1/2 cup white wine vinegar

1/3 cup olive or vegetable oil

1/4 cup balsamic vinegar

1 1/2 teaspoons chopped fresh or 1/2 teaspoon dried basil leaves

1/4 teaspoon coarsely ground pepper

1/8 teaspoon salt

Cook pasta as directed on package; drain. Rinse with cold water; drain. Place beans and pearl onions in 1 inch water in 2-quart saucepan. Heat to boiling; reduce heat. Simmer uncovered 10 to 15 minutes or until crisp-tender; drain. Immediately rinse with cold water; drain.

Mix remaining ingredients. Place pasta, beans and onions and peppers in 8 × 8 inch baking dish, keeping each item separate. Pour dressing mixture over pasta and vegetables. Cover and refrigerate at least 3 hours but no longer than 8 hours, spooning marinade over mixture occasionally. Remove pasta and vegetables from marinade with slotted spoon; discard marinade. Arrange pasta and vegetables on shallow serving platter. Serve with toothpicks.

1 Appetizer: Calories 65 (Calories from Fat 10); Fat 1g (Saturated 0g); Cholesterol 0mg; Sodium 10mg; Carbohydrate 13g (Dietary Fiber 1g); Protein 2g.

Fresh Herb Flavor and Use

Using fresh herbs is fun and easy. If you don't know how to pair herbs with food, the guide below should be a helpful start.

Look for fresh, bright herbs with leaves that are not wilted or discolored. Store in refrigerator until ready to use. Freshly cut herbs that will not be used right away can be refrigerated in plastic bags for 1 to 2 days. Those with larger stems such as basil, mint, tarragon and cilantro can be refrigerated with the stems in a glass of water (keeping the leaves out of the water) for up to five days.

Basil—The sweet flavor is good with tomato dishes, sauces, soups, salads, meats and eggs.

Chives—The mild onion flavor is good with meats, vegetables, pasta, spreads, dips, breads and soups.

Cilantro—The pungent and distinctive flavor is good with Mexican and Asian foods such as salsas, curries and peanut sauces.

Dill Weed—The pungent and tangy flavor is good with breads, cheese, fish, salads, sauces and vegetables.

Marjoram—The flavor is like a mild oregano and is good with meats, vegetables, soups and salads.

Mint—The flavor is cool and sweet and is good with beverages, desserts, fish, lamb, sauces and soups.

Oregano—The strong, slightly bitter flavor is good with tomato dishes, cheese, eggs, fish, meats, sauces, soups and vegetables.

Parsley—The slightly peppery flavor is good in herb mixtures, sauces, soups, stews and as a garnish.

Rosemary—The strong, fresh, sweet flavor is good with bread, vegetables, meats, fish, lamb and salads.

Sage—The strong, slightly bitter flavor is good with stuffing, poultry, meats and fish.

Tarragon—The aniselike flavor is good with poultry, eggs, meat, sauces and salads.

Thyme—The pungent flavor is good with poultry, stuffing, fish, meats, soups, stews and tomato dishes.

ZESTY SHRIMP BITES

60 APPETIZERS

Use a pastry bag with a wide tip to fill the manicotti shells quickly and easily.

6 uncooked manicotti shells

1 package (8 ounces) cream cheese, softened

1/2 cup margarine, butter or spread, softened

1/2 cup mayonnaise or salad dressing

1/4 cup sliced pimiento-stuffed olives

1 1/2 teaspoons red pepper sauce

1/2 cup sliced green onions, including tops (5 medium)

1 package (10 ounces) frozen cooked shrimp, thawed, drained and chopped

Cook and drain manicotti as directed on package; pat dry. Place remaining ingredients in food processor. Cover and process about 30 seconds or until smooth.

Fill manicotti with cream cheese mixture. Place in shallow container. Cover tightly with plastic wrap and refrigerate about 2 hours or until firm.

Cut manicotti into about 1/2-inch slices. Arrange slices on serving plate. Sprinkle with additional sliced green onions if desired.

1 Appetizer: Calories 50 (Calories from Fat 35); Fat 4g (Saturated 1g); Cholesterol 10mg; Sodium 65mg; Carbohydrate 2g (Dietary Fiber 0g); Protein 1g.

ANTIPASTO PASTA

6 SERVINGS

This beautiful cold salad is based on the classic Italian appetizer antipasto. It makes a great first course.

3 cups uncooked farfalle (bow-tie) pasta
   (about 8 ounces)

1/4 cup red wine vinegar

1 tablespoon finely chopped fresh or
   1 teaspoon dried basil leaves

1 tablespoon capers

2 tablespoons olive or vegetable oil

1/4 teaspoon garlic powder

1/2 cup cubed mozzarella cheese
   (2 ounces)

1/2 cup chopped drained pepperoncini
   peppers

1/4 cup ripe olives, halved

1/4 cup (1 ounce) sliced pepperoni (about
   20 slices)

1 medium red bell pepper, cut into
   2 × 1/4-inch strips

1/2 medium zucchini, cut lengthwise in
   half, then crosswise into 1/4-inch
   slices (about 1/2 cup)

1 package (9ounces) frozen artichoke
   hearts, thawed and quartered

Cook and drain pasta as directed on package. Rinse with cold water; drain. Mix vinegar, basil, capers, oil and garlic powder. Toss pasta, vinegar mixture and remaining ingredients. Cover and refrigerate about 1 hour or until chilled.

1 Serving: Calories 260 (Calories from Fat 100); Fat 11g (Saturated 3g); Cholesterol 45mg; Sodium 410 mg; Carbohydrate 33g (Dietary Fiber 4 g); Protein 11g.

3

MEAT

*Pasta Bundles
with Chèvre
(p.65)*

BEEF GOULASH

6 SERVINGS

1 1/2 pounds ground beef

1 medium onion, chopped (1/2 cup)

1 medium stalk celery, sliced (1/2 cup)

1 can (16 ounces) stewed tomatoes, undrained

1 package (7 ounces) elbow macaroni (2 cups)

1 can (6 ounces) tomato paste

2 cups water

2 teaspoons Worcestershire sauce

1/2 teaspoon pepper

1/4 teaspoon salt

Heat oven to 350°. Cook beef, onion and celery in ovenproof Dutch oven over medium-high heat, stirring occasionally, until beef is brown; drain. Stir in remaining ingredients.

Cover and bake 40 to 50 minutes or until liquid is absorbed and goulash is hot.

1 Serving: Calories 395 (Calories from Fat 155); Fat 17g (Saturated 7g); Cholesterol 65mg; Sodium 510mg; Carbohydrate 37g (Dietary Fiber 3g); Protein 27g.

BURGUNDY BEEF

8 SERVINGS

1 1/2 pounds beef round steak, 1 inch thick

2 tablespoons vegetable oil

4 large onions, sliced

6 cups sliced mushrooms (1 pound)

3 tablespoons all-purpose flour

2 teaspoons salt

1 teaspoon chopped fresh or 1/4 teaspoon dried marjoram leaves

1 teaspoon chopped fresh or 1/4 teaspoon dried thyme leaves

1/4 teaspoon pepper

1 cup beef broth

2 cups red Burgundy or other dry red wine (or nonalcoholic) or beef broth

8 cups hot cooked egg noodles

Cut beef into 1-inch cubes. Heat oil in Dutch oven over medium-high heat. Cook beef in oil, stirring occasionally, until brown. Remove beef from Dutch oven.

Cook onions and mushrooms in Dutch oven over medium-high heat, stirring occasionally, until onions are tender. Remove mushrooms and onions from Dutch oven; cover and refrigerate.

Return beef to Dutch oven. Sprinkle with flour, salt, marjoram, thyme and pepper. Stir in broth and Burgundy. Heat to boiling; reduce heat to low. Cover and simmer about 1 1/4 hours or until beef is tender. (Liquid should just cover beef; if necessary, stir in additional broth or wine.)

Add onions and mushrooms; cook until hot, stirring occasionally. Serve over noodles.

1 Serving: Calories 435 (Calories from Fat 110); Fat 12g (Saturated 3g); Cholesterol 100mg; Sodium 680mg; Carbohydrate 52g (Dietary Fiber 5g); Protein 28g.

BAKED BEEF AND CHEESE MACARONI

6 SERVINGS

A touch of cinnamon and a tomato-beef sauce layer add new dimensions to this Greek version of the versatile macaroni casserole so popular with American budget watchers.

**1 package (7 ounces) elbow macaroni
   (2 cups)**

3/4 pound ground beef

1 small onion, chopped (1/4 cup)

1 can (15 ounces) tomato sauce

1/2 teaspoon salt

**1 1/2 cups grated Parmesan or Romano
   cheese (6 ounces)**

1/8 teaspoon ground cinnamon

1 1/4 cups milk

3 tablespoons margarine, butter or spread

2 eggs, slightly beaten

1/8 teaspoon ground nutmeg

Heat oven to 325°. Grease square baking dish, 8 × 8 × 2 inches. Cook and drain macaroni as directed on package. Cook beef and onion in 10-inch skillet over medium-high heat, stirring occasionally, until beef is brown; drain. Stir in tomato sauce and salt.

Spread half of the macaroni in baking dish. Spread beef mixture over macaroni. Mix 1/2 cup of the cheese and the cinnamon; sprinkle over beef mixture. Spread with remaining macaroni.

Cook milk and margarine in 2-quart saucepan, stirring occasionally, until margarine is melted; remove from heat. Gradually stir at least half of the milk mixture into eggs; stir back into milk mixture in saucepan. Pour over macaroni. Sprinkle with remaining 1 cup cheese.

Bake uncovered 50 to 60 minutes or until top is golden brown and center is set. Sprinkle with nutmeg.

1 Serving: Calories 450 (Calories from Fat 205); Fat 23g (Saturated 10g); Cholesterol 125mg; Sodium 1120mg; Carbohydrate 35g (Dietary Fiber 2g); Protein 28g.

SKILLET SPAGHETTI

6 SERVINGS

A one-pan version of a classic favorite is welcome with today's busy lifestyles. The ingredients remain; the name has been changed to emphasize its added convenience!

1 pound ground beef

1 large onion, chopped (1 cup)

3/4 cup chopped green bell pepper

1/2 cup water

2 teaspoons salt

1 teaspoon sugar

1 teaspoon chili powder

**1 can (28 ounces) whole tomatoes,
   undrained**

**1 package (7 ounces) spaghetti, broken into
   pieces**

**1 can (4 ounces) mushroom stems and
   pieces, drained**

1 cup shredded Cheddar cheese (4 ounces)

Cook beef and onion in 12-inch skillet or Dutch oven until beef is brown; drain. Stir in remaining ingredients except cheese, breaking up tomatoes.

Heat to boiling; reduce heat to low. Cover and simmer about 30 minutes, stirring occasionally, until spaghetti is tender. Sprinkle with cheese. Cover and heat until cheese is melted.

1 Serving: Calories 400 (Calories from Fat 160); Fat 18g (Saturated 8g); Cholesterol 65mg; Sodium 1160mg; Carbohydrate 37g (Dietary Fiber 3g); Protein 25g.

BEEF STROGANOFF

4 SERVINGS

Try using lower fat sour cream to reduce the fat but still retain the rich quality of this traditional favorite. Use a mixture of regular and the more exotic mushrooms to dress it up for entertaining.

1 pound beef tenderloin, boneless top loin or sirloin steak, about 1/2 inch thick

2 tablespoons margarine, butter or spread

3 cups sliced mushrooms (8 ounces)

1 medium onion, thinly sliced

1 small clove garlic, finely chopped

3/4 cup dry red wine (or nonalcoholic) or beef broth

1/2 teaspoon Worcestershire sauce

1 teaspoon salt

1/2 cup beef broth

3 tablespoons all-purpose flour

1 cup sour cream

4 cups hot cooked egg noodles

Cut beef across grain into 1 1/2 × 1/2-inch strips. Melt margarine in 10-inch skillet over medium-high heat. Cook mushrooms, onion and garlic in margarine, stirring occasionally, until onion is tender. Remove mushroom mixture from skillet.

Cook beef in same skillet, stirring occasionally, until brown. Stir in wine, Worcestershire sauce and salt. Heat to boiling; reduce heat to low. Cover and simmer 15 minutes.

Stir broth into flour; stir into beef mixture. Stir in mushroom mixture. Heat to boiling, stirring constantly. Boil and stir 1 minute; reduce heat to low. Stir in sour cream; cook until hot, but do not boil. Serve over noodles.

1 Serving: Calories 620 (Calories from Fat 290); Fat 32g (Saturated 13g); Cholesterol 155mg; Sodium 780mg; Carbohydrate 49g (Dietary Fiber 4g); Protein 33g.

SAUERBRATEN MEATBALLS AND NOODLES

6 SERVINGS

1 pound lean ground beef or pork

1/3 cup crushed gingersnaps (about 6 gingersnaps)

1/2 cup finely chopped onion (about 1 medium)

1/4 cup water

1/2 teaspoon salt

1/4 teaspoon pepper

6 ounces uncooked egg noodles or spaetzle (about 3 cups)

1 cup beef broth

1/4 cup apple cider vinegar

1 tablespoon sugar

1/4 cup crushed gingersnaps (about 4 gingersnaps)

2 tablespoons raisins

Heat oven to 400°. Mix ground beef, 1/3 cup gingersnaps, the onion, water, salt and pepper. Shape mixture into 24 meatballs. Spray rack in broiler pan with nonstick cooking spray. Place meatballs on rack. Bake uncovered 20 to 25 minutes or until done and light brown.

Cook noodles as directed on package; drain. Mix remaining ingredients except raisins in 1 1/2-quart saucepan. Cook over medium heat, stirring constantly, until mixture thickens and boils. Stir in raisins and meatballs. Heat until hot. Serve over noodles.

1 Serving: Calories 320 (Calories from Fat 115); Fat 13g (Saturated 5); Cholesterol 65mg; Sodium 390mg; Carbohydrate 34g (Dietary Fiber 2g); Protein 19g.

Sauerbraten Meatballs and Noodles

SPAGHETTI AND MEATBALLS

6 SERVINGS

Spaghetti and meatballs—nearly everyone's favorite "Italian" dish—is truly international fare. Spaghetti originated in the Orient, meatballs in the Middle East, tomato sauce in Mexico, and the essential Parmesan cheese really does come from Italy—it has been produced in the city of Parma for more than 800 years!

Meatballs (right)
1 tablespoon olive or vegetable oil
1 medium onion, chopped (1/2 cup)
1 clove garlic, finely chopped
1 can (28 ounces) whole tomatoes, undrained
1 can (6 ounces) tomato paste
1/4 cup chopped fresh parsley
1/4 cup water
1 teaspoon sugar
1 teaspoon salt
1/2 teaspoon dried basil leaves
1/4 teaspoon pepper
1 package (16 ounces) spaghetti
Grated Parmesan cheese

Prepare Meatballs. Heat oil in Dutch oven over medium-high heat. Cook onion and garlic in oil, stirring occasionally, until onion is tender.

Stir in remaining ingredients except spaghetti and cheese, breaking up tomatoes. Heat to boiling; reduce heat to low. Cover and simmer 30 minutes, stirring occasionally.

Add meatballs to sauce. Cover and simmer 15 minutes. Cook and drain spaghetti as directed on package. Place spaghetti on large platter. Top with meatballs and sauce. Sprinkle with cheese.

MEATBALLS

1 1/2 pounds ground beef
3/4 cup dry bread crumbs
1/2 cup milk
2 tablespoons grated Parmesan cheese
1 tablespoon chopped fresh parsley
1 teaspoon salt
1/2 teaspoon dried oregano leaves
1/4 teaspoon pepper
1 medium onion, finely chopped (1/2 cup)
1 egg

Heat oven to 350°. Mix all ingredients. Shape mixture into 1 1/2-inch balls. Place in ungreased jelly roll pan, 15 × 10 1/2 × 1 inch. Bake uncovered 15 to 20 minutes or until beef is no longer pink in center and juice is clear.

1 Serving: Calories 700 (Calories from Fat 215); Fat 24g (Saturated 9g); Cholesterol 105mg; Sodium 1470mg; Carbohydrate 87g (Dietary Fiber 6g); Protein 40g.

Beef Fillets with Fettuccine and Green Peppercorn-Mustard Sauce

4 SERVINGS

To grind peppercorns, place them in a plastic bag, seal bag and pound on hard surface with a rolling pin, or grind peppercorns in a food processor, using short on-and-off motions.

1 tablespoon margarine, butter or spread

4 six-ounce beef tenderloin steaks

4 ounces uncooked fettuccine

4 ounces uncooked spinach fettuccine

1 tablespoon margarine, butter or spread

2 cups whipping (heavy) cream

3 tablespoons Dijon mustard

2 tablespoons whole green peppercorns, coarsely ground

1 tablespoon whole green peppercorns

Melt 1 tablespoon margarine in 10-inch skillet over medium heat. Cook beef in margarine about 7 minutes on each side, turning once, until brown. Remove beef from skillet.

Cook and drain fettuccines as directed on package. Toss fettuccines and 1 tablespoon margarine.

Mix whipping cream, mustard and ground and whole peppercorns in same skillet. Heat to boiling; reduce heat to medium-low. Simmer uncovered about 5 to 8 minutes, stirring occasionally and scraping any brown bits off the bottom of the skillet, until thickened.

Return beef and any juices to skillet. Cover and simmer over low heat about 12 minutes for medium doneness, or until desired doneness. Arrange fettuccines on dinner plates. Serve with beef and peppercorn sauce.

1 Serving: Calories 825 (Calories from Fat 505); Fat 56g (Saturated 29g); Cholesterol 265mg; Sodium 330mg; Carbohydrate 42g (Dietary Fiber 3g); Protein 41g.

New Tomato Products

Traditional canned tomato products such as tomato sauce, tomato paste and whole tomatoes are being joined by many new products. These new products offer tremendous flavor, versatility and convenience. Among the choices are Italian- and Mexican-flavored chunky tomato mixtures along with flavored tomato sauce and stewed tomatoes. Several of the recipes in this book use these new products. In the grocery store, they can generally be found in one of the following areas: canned tomato products, spaghetti sauces or canned vegetables.

EASY SESAME BEEF

4 SERVINGS

1 pound beef boneless sirloin steak

2 tablespoons sugar

2 tablespoons soy sauce

1/4 teaspoon pepper

**1/4 cup finely chopped green onions
(3 medium)**

2 cloves garlic, finely chopped

1 tablespoon sesame seed

2 tablespoons vegetable oil

2 cups hot cooked vermicelli

Cut beef diagonally across grain into 1/8-inch slices. (Beef is easier to cut if partially frozen, about 1 1/2 hours.) Mix sugar, soy sauce, pepper, onions and garlic in glass or plastic bowl. Stir in beef until well coated. Cover and refrigerate 30 minutes.

Drain beef mixture. Heat sesame seed in 10-inch skillet over medium heat, stirring frequently, until golden brown. Remove sesame seed from skillet.

Heat oil in same skillet over medium-high heat. Cook beef mixture in oil, stirring occasionally, until brown. Serve over vermicelli. Sprinkle with sesame seed.

1 Serving: Calories 300 (Calories from Fat 100); Fat 11g (Saturated 2g); Cholesterol 55mg; Sodium 560mg; Carbohydrate 27g (Dietary Fiber 1g); Protein 24g.

STIR-FRIED ASIAN BEEF AND NOODLES

6 SERVINGS

Asian cuisine is masterful at combining colors, textures and flavors for a satisfying, enjoyable meal. The frozen vegetables save some chopping time and can be customized to your liking.

1 pound beef boneless sirloin or round steak

1 tablespoon vegetable oil

1 teaspoon cornstarch

1/2 teaspoon soy sauce

1 package (about 6 ounces) rice stick noodles

1 tablespoon vegetable oil

1 tablespoon finely chopped gingerroot

1 clove garlic, finely chopped

1 package (16 ounces) frozen broccoli, carrots, water chestnuts and red peppers, thawed

1 tablespoon vegetable oil

3/4 cup beef broth

1/3 cup rice or cider vinegar

1/3 cup honey

3 tablespoons soy sauce

1 teaspoon sesame oil

1/4 teaspoon crushed red pepper

1/4 cup sliced green onions (3 medium)

Cut beef into 2 × 1/4-inch strips. Toss beef, 1 tablespoon vegetable oil, the cornstarch and 1/2 teaspoon soy sauce in glass or plastic bowl. Cover and refrigerate 20 minutes. Soak noodles in cold water 5 minutes; drain.

Heat wok or 12-inch skillet over medium-high heat until hot. Add 1 tablespoon vegetable oil; rotate skillet to coat side. Add gingerroot and garlic; stir-fry 30 seconds. Add vegetables; stir-fry until crisp-tender. Remove vegetables from wok.

Add 1 tablespoon vegetable oil to wok; rotate to coat side. Add beef; stir-fry until brown. Remove beef from wok.

Add broth, vinegar, honey, 3 tablespoons soy sauce, sesame oil and the red pepper to wok. Stir in noodles; heat to boiling. Cook over medium heat about 2 minutes, stirring frequently, until noodles are tender. Stir in beef, vegetables and onions; cook and stir 1 minute.

1 Serving: Calories 300 (Calories from Fat 90); Fat 10g (Saturated 2g); Cholesterol 35mg; Sodium 680mg; Carbohydrate 38g (Dietary Fiber 2g); Protein 17g.

RAITA PASTA WITH SPICY STEAK

4 SERVINGS

This Indian-influenced dish takes Raita—the typical yogurt-chopped vegetable accompaniment—and adds a pasta twist.

Spicy Rub (below)

1/2 pound beef flank steak

1 1/2 cups uncooked gemelli (twists) pasta (6 ounces)

1 cup plain yogurt

1/2 large tomato, seeded and diced (1/2 cup)

1/2 medium cucumber, seeded and diced (1/2 cup)

1/4 cup chopped fresh cilantro or parsley

1/4 teaspoon salt

Prepare Spicy Rub; rub mixture on both sides of beef. Cover and refrigerate 1 hour.

Cook and drain pasta as directed on package. Mix yogurt, tomato, cucumber, cilantro and salt in large bowl; toss with pasta.

Set oven control to broil. Grease broiler pan rack. Place beef on rack in broiler pan. Broil with top about 3 inches from heat about 5 minutes or until brown. Turn beef; broil 4 to 6 minutes longer for medium doneness or until desired doneness. Cut beef diagonally into very thin slices. Serve with pasta mixture.

SPICY RUB

1 1/2 teaspoons olive or vegetable oil

1/2 teaspoon ground cumin

1/4 teaspoon crushed red pepper

1/4 teaspoon salt

1/8 teaspoon ground red pepper (cayenne)

1/8 teaspoon chili powder

1 clove garlic, finely chopped

Mix all ingredients.

To Grill: Grill rubbed beef uncovered 4 to 5 inches from medium coals 6 to 8 minutes on each side for medium doneness, turning occasionally, or until desired doneness.

1 Serving: Calories 295 (Calories from Fat 65); Fat 7g (Saturated 2g); Cholesterol 35mg; Sodium 340mg; Carbohydrate 39g (Dietary Fiber 1g); Protein 20g.

TERIYAKI BEEF STIR-FRY

6 SERVINGS

1 pound ground beef

2 teaspoons soy sauce

1 teaspoon finely chopped gingerroot

1/4 cup sliced green onions (3 medium)

1 clove garlic, finely chopped

1 small red bell pepper, thinly sliced

1/2 large red onion, thinly sliced

2 stalks bok choy, cut into 1-inch slices (1 cup)

1 cup teriyaki barbecue marinade

1 package (8 ounces) uncooked Chinese noodles or spaghetti

Mix beef, soy sauce, 1/2 teaspoon of the ginger-root, the green onions and garlic. Shape mixture into 1-inch balls. Cook over medium-high heat about 6 minutes, turning occasionally, until beef is no longer pink in center and juice is clear. Remove meatballs from skillet; keep warm. Drain drippings from skillet, reserving 1 tablespoon.

Cook remaining 1/2 teaspoon gingerroot in drippings in skillet over medium-high heat 30 seconds. Add bell pepper, red onion and bok choy. Cook, stirring occasionally, until crisp-tender. Stir in teriyaki barbecue marinade. Stir in meatballs; cook until hot.

Cook and drain noodles as directed on package. Serve meatball mixture over noodles.

1 Serving: Calories 285 (Calories from Fat 100); Fat 11g (Saturated 4g); Cholesterol 45mg; Sodium 2000mg; Carbohydrate 30g (Dietary Fiber 1g); Protein 18g.

MEXICAN LASAGNA

8 SERVINGS

1 package (8 ounces) lasagna noodles

1 pound lean ground beef

1 medium onion, chopped (1/2 cup)

1/4 cup chopped fresh cilantro

2 teaspoons chili powder

1 container (15 ounces) ricotta cheese

1 jar (24 ounces) salsa

1 cup shredded Monterey Jack cheese (4 ounces)

Heat oven to 375°. Cook and drain noodles as directed on package. Cook beef, onion, cilantro and chili powder in 10-inch skillet over medium heat, stirring occasionally, until beef is brown; drain.

Place 5 of the noodles in bottom of ungreased rectangular pan, 13 × 9 × 2 inches. Layer with 1 1/2 cups of the beef mixture, 1 cup of the ricotta cheese and 1 1/4 cups of the salsa. Repeat with remaining noodles, beef mixture, ricotta cheese and salsa. Sprinkle with Monterey Jack cheese.

Bake uncovered 35 to 40 minutes or until hot. Let stand 10 minutes before cutting.

1 Serving: Calories 375 (Calories from Fat 160); Fat 18g (Saturated 9g); Cholesterol 60mg; Sodium 690mg; Carbohydrate 31g (Dietary Fiber 3g); Protein 25g.

GRILLED BEEF AND CALICO PASTA

6 SERVINGS

1/2 pound beef flank steak

1 1/2 cups Italian dressing

8 ounces uncooked linguine

1 jalapeño chile, seeded

2 cloves garlic

1 can (15 to 16 ounces) kidney beans, drained

1/2 teaspoon paprika

1/4 teaspoon chili powder

Dash of red pepper sauce

1/2 cup canned black beans, rinsed and drained

1/2 cup whole kernel corn, drained

3 tablespoons chopped fresh cilantro or parsley

Cut diamond pattern 1/8 inch deep into both sides of beef. Place beef in shallow glass or plastic dish. Pour 1 cup of the dressing over beef. Cover and refrigerate at least 4 hours but no longer than 24 hours, turning occasionally.

Cook and drain linguine as directed on package. Place chile and garlic in blender or food processor. Cover and blend on until finely chopped. Add kidney beans, remaining dressing, the paprika, chili powder and pepper sauce. Cover and blend until almost smooth; set aside.

Remove beef from marinade; reserve marinade. Grill beef uncovered 4 to 5 inches from medium coals 6 to 8 minutes for medium or until desired doneness, turning and brushing with marinade once. Discard marinade.

Cut beef diagonally across the grain into thin slices. Mix black beans, corn and cilantro. Top linguine with kidney bean mixture, black bean mixture and beef. Sprinkle with chopped fresh cilantro if desired.

To Broil: Set oven control to broil. Grease broiler pan rack. Place marinated beef on rack in broiler pan. Brush with marinade. Broil with top about 3 inches from heat about 5 minutes or until brown. Turn beef; broil 4 to 6 minutes longer for medium doneness or until desired doneness.

1 Serving: Calories 360 (Calories from Fat 115); Fat 13g (Saturated 3g); Cholesterol 25mg; Sodium 430mg; Carbohydrate 49g (Dietary Fiber 6g); Protein 18g.

GREEK BEEF AND COUSCOUS

4 SERVINGS

1 tablespoon olive or vegetable oil

1 pound beef boneless sirloin, cut into
  1-inch pieces

1 medium onion, chopped (1/2 cup)

2 cloves garlic, finely chopped

1 1/2 cups beef broth

3/4 cup uncooked couscous

5 roma (plum) tomatoes, coarsely chopped
  (2 cups)

2 tablespoons chopped fresh or 2 teaspoons
  dried oregano leaves

1/4 teaspoon pepper

2 ounces crumbled feta cheese (1/2 cup)

Heat oil in 10-inch skillet over medium-high heat. Cook beef, onion and garlic in oil, stirring occasionally, until beef is brown. Stir in broth; heat to boiling.

Stir in couscous, tomatoes, oregano and pepper; remove from heat. Cover and let stand 10 minutes or until liquid is absorbed. Top with cheese.

1 Serving: Calories 340 (Calories from Fat 90); Fat 10g (Saturated 4g); Cholesterol 65mg; Sodium 450mg; Carbohydrate 36g (Dietary Fiber 3g); Protein 30g.

VENEZUELAN ROLL-UPS

8 SERVINGS

1/2 recipe Cornmeal Pasta (page 20) or
  8 uncooked lasagna noodles

1 pound ground beef

1 jar (16 ounces) hot thick-and-chunky salsa

1 small green bell pepper, chopped (1/2 cup)

1 medium onion, chopped (1/2 cup)

1/2 cup sliced pimiento-stuffed olives

3 cups shredded Colby cheese (12 ounces)

1 1/3 cups sour cream

Heat oven to 350°. Prepare dough for Cornmeal Pasta and roll as directed on page 22. Cut into lasagna noodles, 11 × 2 3/4 inches. Cook and drain as directed on page 23. (If using dry uncooked lasagne noodles, cook and drain as directed on package.)

Cook beef in 10-inch skillet over medium-high heat, stirring occasionally, until beef is brown; drain. Stir in 1 cup of the salsa, the bell pepper, onion and olives; cook until hot.

Mix 1 cup of the cheese and the sour cream. Spread about 1 1/2 tablespoons cheese mixture over one side of each noodle. Spread with about 2/3 cup beef mixture. Sprinkle each with remaining cheese.

Roll up loosely, beginning at narrow end. Place rolls, seam sides down, in ungreased rectangular baking dish, 13 × 9 × 2 inches. Spread remaining salsa over rolls. Cover tightly and bake about 30 minutes or until hot.

1 Serving: Calories 425 (Calories from Fat 260); Fat 29g (Saturated 16g); Cholesterol 110mg; Sodium 1000mg; Carbohydrate 23g (Dietary Fiber 3g); Protein 21g.

CHEESY BARBECUE CASSEROLE

6 SERVINGS

**3 cups uncooked ziti or penne pasta
   (8 ounces)**

1 pound ground beef

1 medium onion, chopped (1/2 cup)

1/4 cup chopped fresh parsley, if desired

1 cup milk

1 cup barbecue sauce

1 cup shredded mozzarella cheese (4 ounces)

**1 1/2 cups shredded Cheddar cheese
   (6 ounces)**

Heat oven to 350°. Cook and drain pasta as directed on package. Grease 2-quart casserole. Cook beef and onion in 10-inch skillet over medium-high heat, stirring occasionally, until beef is brown; drain. Mix beef and remaining ingredients except 1/2 cup of the Cheddar cheese. Spoon into casserole. Sprinkle with 1/2 cup Cheddar cheese. Bake uncovered 30 to 40 minutes or until hot and bubbly.

1 Serving: Calories 530 (Calories from Fat 235); Fat 26g (Saturated 13g); Cholesterol 90mg; Sodium 690mg; Carbohydrate 41g (Dietary Fiber 2g); Protein 35g.

EASY SOUTHWESTERN STROGANOFF

4 SERVINGS

1 pound ground beef

1 cup water

1 jar (16 ounces) thick-and-chunky salsa

**2 cups uncooked wagon wheel pasta
   (4 ounces)**

1/2 teaspoon salt

1/2 cup sour cream

Cook beef in 10-inch skillet over medium-high heat, stirring occasionally, until brown; drain. Stir in water, salsa, pasta and salt. Heat to boiling; reduce heat to low.

Cover and simmer about 15 minutes, stirring occasionally, until pasta is tender. Stir in sour cream; cook just until hot.

1 Serving: Calories 405 (Calories from Fat 205); Fat 23g (Saturated 10g); Cholesterol 85mg; Sodium 990mg; Carbohydrate 27g (Dietary Fiber 3g); Protein 26g.

CASUAL PASTA PARTY

Entertaining at home is a great way to see friends or meet new people. If the idea of relaxing at your own party prompts you to say, "no way," our Pasta Party idea will change your mind and make you a believer in the concept of "potluck" entertaining. Potluck can mean two things. On one hand, it means bringing whatever you choose, even if a request has been made for a specific food type such as an appetizer or dessert. It can also mean that you assign a specific food or recipe such as garlic bread or chocolate chip cookies. Assigning specifics allows the party planner control over the menu, yet allows guests flexibility in contributing their favorite recipe or food. In fact, this casual approach to entertaining is far more popular than the formal dinner parties of the past. And with good reason—it's easy and fun!

The Pasta Party suggested below is for eight people. Ask each person or couple to bring a specific item or send them a copy of the recipe you would like them to prepare.

Plan to serve the food buffet-style so your guests can "mix-and-match" their own pasta and sauces. Start the line with plates and bowls, then follow with the pastas, sauces and toppings. The bread, salad and silverware can be placed either on the dining table or at the end of the buffet line so guests won't have to juggle them while making their pasta creations.

PASTAS: (CHOOSE ANY ONE OF THE FOLLOWING TO EQUAL EIGHT CUPS OF HOT COOKED PASTA)

- Fettuccine, linguine, spaghetti or other long, thin pasta
- Penne, mostaccioli, rigatoni, rotini or other tubular or spiral pasta
- Tortellini, ravioli or other filled pasta

SAUCES: (CHOOSE ONE OR MORE)

- Alfredo Sauce (page 132)
- Basil Pesto (page 142)
- Bolognese Sauce (page 144)

TOPPINGS: (CHOOSE ONE OR MORE)

Hot cooked bulk or link Italian sausage

Diced fully cooked smoked ham

Crisply cooked and crumbled bacon

Grilled chicken breast pieces

Sliced ripe olives

Chopped tomatoes

Capers, drained

Chopped fresh basil or parsley

Freshly ground pepper

Crushed red pepper flakes

Freshly shredded Parmesan cheese

SALAD AND BREAD: (CHOOSE ONE OR MORE)

Eight cups tossed salad greens, assorted bottled dressings and croutons

Garlic bread (purchased or homemade)

Olive Crostini (page 175)

Artichoke Rosemary Bruschetta (page 177)

Pesto Parmesan Loaf (page 176)

LAYERED PASTA PIE

8 SERVINGS

The colors of the Italian flag are all here when you slice into this easy yet elegant pie. If you wish, decorate the top crust with the leftover pastry.

1 cup uncooked elbow macaroni (3 1/2 ounces)

1 cup small curd creamed cottage cheese

1/2 cup grated Parmesan cheese

1 teaspoon Italian seasoning

1 pound ground beef

1 cup spaghetti sauce

1 package (17 1/4 ounces) frozen puff pastry, thawed

1 1/2 cups mozzarella cheese (6 ounces)

1 package (12 ounces) frozen spinach soufflé, thawed

Move oven rack to lowest position. Heat oven to 425°. Grease springform pan, 9 × 3 inches. Cook and drain macaroni as directed on package. Toss macaroni, cottage cheese, Parmesan cheese and Italian seasoning.

Cook beef in 10-inch skillet over medium-high heat, stirring occasionally, until brown; drain. Stir in spaghetti sauce.

Roll each sheet of puff pastry into 14-inch square on lightly floured surface. Fit one of the sheets in bottom and up side of springform pan. Trim overhanging edge of pastry 1/2 inch from edge of pan. Layer beef mixture, 1/2 cup of the mozzarella cheese and the macaroni mixture in pan; press lightly with back of spoon. Layer 1/2 cup of the mozzarella cheese, the spinach soufflé and the remaining 1/2 cup mozzarella cheese on macaroni mixture.

Top with second sheet of pastry. Trim overhanging edge of pastry 1 inch from rim of pan. Fold and roll top edge over lower edge of pastry, pressing edges together inside rim of pan. Flute as desired. Cut slits in top pastry for steam to escape.

Bake 25 to 30 minutes or until top is golden brown. Cool in pan on wire rack 15 minutes; carefully remove side of pan. Let pie stand 15 minutes before cutting into wedges.

1 Serving: Calories 735 (Calories from Fat 460); Fat 51g (Saturated 20g); Cholesterol 110mg; Sodium 880mg; Carbohydrate 42g (Dietary Fiber 2g); Protein 29g.

OLIVE PESTO PASTA

6 SERVINGS

1 jar (10 ounces) garlic or pimiento-stuffed green olives, drained

1 cup firmly packed parsley sprigs

1/3 cup olive or vegetable oil

1/3 cup beef broth

1/8 teaspoon pepper

4 cups uncooked mafalde (mini-lasagna noodle) pasta (8 ounces)

2 medium carrots, cut into thin julienne strips

3 cups cut-up roast beef (about 1 pound)

Place olives and parsley in food processor or blender. Cover and process until finely chopped. Add oil, broth and pepper. Cover and process until mixture is smooth.

Cook pasta as directed on package, adding carrots 3 minutes before pasta is done; drain. Toss with olive pesto and roast beef.

1 Serving: Calories 450 (Calories from Fat 250); Fat 28g (Saturated 6g); Cholesterol 55mg; Sodium 1000mg; Carbohydrate 26g (Dietary Fiber 2g); Protein 24g.

PASTA BUNDLES WITH CHÈVRE

6 SERVINGS

1/2 recipe Cornmeal Pasta (page 20) or Fresh Pasta (page 18)

1/2 pound ground beef

6 ounces chèvre (goat) cheese or cream cheese

1 jar (1 3/4 ounces) pine nuts, chopped (1/3 cup)

12 whole chives (about 8 inches long)

2 cups half-and-half

2 tablespoons all-purpose flour

1/2 teaspoon salt

1 tablespoon grated orange peel

1 tablespoon chopped fresh chives

1 tablespoon chopped fresh or 1 teaspoon dried basil leaves

Prepare dough for Cornmeal Pasta. Divide into 6 equal pieces and roll dough as directed on page 22 into 11 × 5 1/2-inch rectangles about 1/16 thick. Cut each rectangle crosswise into squares. Cover squares with plastic wrap until ready to use.

Cook ground beef in small skillet over medium-high heat until brown; drain. Stir in 2 ounces of the goat cheese and pine nuts.

Using 1 heaping tablespoon beef mixture, place 1 mound in center of each square. Moisten dough lightly around mounds with water. Fold dough up and over mounds; pinch dough on each side of mounds to seal. Place whole chives in boiling water just until limp; drain.

Tie pinched areas with chives to form bundles. Place on lightly floured towel; sprinkle lightly with flour. Repeat with remaining beef mixture and squares. Cover rectangles with plastic wrap until ready to use.

Meanwhile, combine half-and-half, flour and salt in 2-quart saucepan. Heat to boiling, stirring frequently. Boil 1 minute, stirring constantly. Remove from heat. Stir in remaining 4 ounces of the goat cheese, orange peel, 1 tablespoon chives and the basil until cheese is melted and mixture is smooth; remove from heat and keep warm.

Heat 4 quarts water to boiling in Dutch oven. Add pasta bundles. Boil about 10 minutes or until bundles are firm but tender. Begin testing for doneness when bundles rise to surface of water. Drain bundles. Spoon about 1/2 cup of the sauce onto each of 6 dinner plates. Top each with 2 pasta bundles.

1 Serving: Calories 485 (Calories from Fat 290); Fat 32g (Saturated 15g); Cholesterol 115mg; Sodium 600mg; Carbohydrate 30g (Dietary Fiber 2g); Protein 21g.

VEAL-PASTA STEW

8 SERVINGS

2 to 4 tablespoons olive or vegetable oil

2 pounds veal stew meat

1 large onion, coarsely chopped (1 cup)

5 cloves garlic, finely chopped

3 cups chicken broth

2 cups eight-vegetable juice

**1 cup dry white wine (or nonalcoholic)
or chicken broth**

**1 tablespoon chopped fresh or 1 teaspoon
dried rosemary leaves**

**1 tablespoon chopped fresh or 1 teaspoon
dried oregano leaves**

1/2 teaspoon salt

1/2 teaspoon pepper

4 medium carrots, sliced (2 cups)

**3 cups uncooked medium pasta shells
(8 ounces)**

1 medium zucchini, sliced (2 cups)

1/2 cup cold water

2 tablespoons all-purpose flour

Heat 2 tablespoons of the oil in Dutch oven over medium-high heat. Cook half of the veal in oil, stirring occasionally, until brown on all sides. Remove veal from Dutch oven; drain. Cook remaining veal in Dutch oven (add 1 tablespoon of the oil if necessary) until brown on all sides. Remove veal from Dutch oven; drain.

Heat remaining 1 tablespoon oil in Dutch oven over medium heat. Cook onion and garlic in oil, stirring occasionally, until onion is tender. Stir in veal, broth, vegetable juice, wine, rosemary, oregano, salt, pepper and carrots. Heat to boiling; reduce heat to low. Cover and simmer about 1 hour or until veal is tender.

Stir in pasta. Heat to boiling; reduce heat to low. Cover and simmer 10 minutes. Stir in zucchini. Cover and simmer about 5 minutes or until pasta and zucchini are tender. Mix water and flour; stir into veal mixture. Simmer 1 minute, stirring constantly, until slightly thickened.

1 Serving: Calories 395 (Calories from Fat 110); Fat 12g (Saturated 4g); Cholesterol 65mg; Sodium 720mg; Carbohydrate 50g (Dietary Fiber 4g); Protein 26g.

MOSTACCIOLI WITH PROSCIUTTO AND PINE NUTS

4 SERVINGS

**3 cups uncooked mostaccioli pasta
(8 ounces)**

1/4 cup margarine, butter or spread

1/2 cup sliced green onions (5 medium)

1/4 cup pine nuts or slivered almonds

1/2 teaspoon herb-seasoned salt

**4 ounces prosciutto or thinly sliced fully
cooked smoked ham, cut into thin strips**

1 cup shredded Parmesan cheese

Cook and drain pasta as directed on package. Melt margarine in 10-inch skillet over medium heat. Cook onions, pine nuts and seasoned salt in margarine, stirring occasionally, until onions are tender.

Toss onion mixture, prosciutto, 1/2 cup of the cheese and the hot mostaccioli. Sprinkle with remaining cheese.

1 Serving: Calories 505 (Calories from Fat 260); Fat 29g (Saturated 10g); Cholesterol 35mg; Sodium 1000mg; Carbohydrate 79g (Dietary Fiber 4g); Protein 29g.

GRILLED ITALIAN SAUSAGE KABOBS

6 SERVINGS

1 1/2 pounds Italian sausage links, cut into 1 1/2-inch pieces

2 medium zucchini, cut into 1-inch pieces

1 medium red bell pepper, cut into 1 1/2-inch pieces

1 medium green bell pepper, cut into 1 1/2-inch pieces

6 large pimiento-stuffed olives

1/2 cup pizza sauce

6 cups hot cooked pasta (any variety)

Cook sausage in 10-inch skillet over medium heat about 10 minutes, stirring occasionally, until partially cooked; drain. Thread sausage, zucchini and bell peppers alternately on each of six 12-inch metal skewers, leaving space between each piece. Place olive on tip of each skewer.

Cover and grill kabobs 5 to 6 inches from medium coals 20 to 25 minutes, turning and brushing 2 or 3 times with pizza sauce, until sausage is no longer pink in center and vegetables are crisp-tender. Serve over pasta, and if desired, with additional pizza sauce.

Broiled Italian Sausage Kabobs: Prepare kabobs as directed. Set oven control to broil. Place kabobs on rack in broiler pan. Broil with tops about 5 inches from heat about 10 minutes, turning and brushing 2 or 3 times with pizza sauce, until sausage is no longer pink in center and vegetables are tender.

1 Serving: Calories 580 (Calories from Fat 290); Fat 32g (Saturated 11g); Cholesterol 90mg; Sodium 1250mg; Carbohydrate 46g (Dietary Fiber 3g); Protein 30g.

SAUSAGE-MUSHROOM PASTA CALZONES

6 SERVINGS

Stuff egg roll wrappers with delicious fillings, and you've got individual pasta pockets without a lot of work!

1/2 pound bulk pork sausage

1 small onion, chopped (1/4 cup)

1 cup spaghetti sauce

6 square egg roll wrappers (about 6 1/2 inches square)

1/2 cup sliced mushrooms

1 cup shredded mozzarella cheese (4 ounces)

1/4 cup crumbled Gorgonzola cheese, if desired

Heat oven to 400°. Grease rectangular baking dish, 13 × 9 × 2 inches. Cook sausage and onion in 10-inch skillet over medium-high heat, stirring occasionally, until sausage is no longer pink; drain. Stir in spaghetti sauce; cook until hot.

Spoon sausage mixture on half of each egg roll wrapper to within 1/2 inch of edge. Top with mushrooms, 1/2 cup of the mozzarella cheese and the Gorgonzola cheese. Moisten edges of wrappers lightly with water. Fold over filling; press edges to seal. Place in baking dish.

Sprinkle with remaining mozzarella cheese. Bake uncovered 15 to 20 minutes or until calzones are hot and cheese begins to brown. Serve with additional spaghetti sauce if desired.

1 Serving: Calories 295 (Calories from Fat 110); Fat 12g (Saturated 5g); Cholesterol 30mg; Sodium 1030mg; Carbohydrate 34g (Dietary Fiber 2g); Protein 15g.

Sausage-Mushroom Pasta Calzones

CHORIZO RAVIOLI WITH ROASTED RED PEPPER CREAM

6 SERVINGS

1/2 recipe Fresh Pasta (page 18) or Roasted Red Bell Pepper Pasta (page 21)

1/2 pound bulk chorizo or Italian sausage

1/3 cup grated Parmesan cheese

1 egg, slightly beaten

1 jar (7 ounces) roasted red bell peppers, undrained

1 small onion, coarsely chopped (1/4 cup)

1 cup whipping (heavy) cream

1 tablespoon chopped fresh or 1 teaspoon dried basil leaves

1/4 teaspoon coarsely ground pepper

1/4 cup shredded Parmesan cheese

1/2 cup chopped walnuts

Prepare dough for Fresh Pasta and roll as directed on page 22. Cut into 5 rectangles, 14 × 4 inches. Cover rectangles with plastic wrap until ready to use.

Cook sausage in 8-inch skillet over medium-high heat, stirring occasionally, until no longer pink; drain. Cool 5 minutes.

Stir 1/3 cup grated cheese and the egg into sausage, breaking up sausage with spoon. Spoon sausage mixture by teaspoonfuls into mounds about 1 1/2 inches apart in 2 rows of 6 mounds on one of the rectangles. Moisten dough lightly around mounds with water; top with second rectangle. Press gently around mounds to seal.

Cut between mounds into 12 squares with pastry cutter or knife. Place on lightly floured towel; sprinkle lightly with flour. Repeat with remaining sausage mixture and rectangles. (For fifth rectangle, cut crosswise in half. Place 6 mounds of sausage mixture on one half of the rectangle. Moisten dough lightly around mounds with water; top with second half of the rectangle. Press gently around mounds to seal. Continue as directed.) Cover rectangles with plastic wrap until ready to use.

Heat bell peppers and onion to boiling in 1-quart saucepan; reduce heat to low. Simmer uncovered about 5 minutes or until mixture is soft. Carefully pour into blender. Cover and blend until smooth. Pour back into saucepan. Stir in whipping cream, basil and pepper. Heat over low heat, stirring occasionally, just until hot; remove from heat and keep warm.

Heat 4 quarts water to boiling in Dutch oven. Add ravioli. Boil uncovered about 6 minutes, stirring occasionally, until firm but tender. Begin testing for doneness when ravioli rise to surface of water. Drain ravioli. Spoon sauce over ravioli. Sprinkle with 1/4 cup shredded cheese and the walnuts.

1 Serving: Calories 555 (Calories from Fat 350); Fat 39g (Saturated 16g); Cholesterol 210mg; Sodium 710mg; Carbohydrate 31g (Dietary Fiber 2g); Protein 22g.

Chorizo Ravioli with Roasted Red Pepper Cream

PORK WITH LINGUINE AND MUSHROOM-BLUE CHEESE SAUCE

4 SERVINGS

1 tablespoon margarine, butter or spread

1 pound pork tenderloin, cut into 1-inch slices

4 ounces uncooked linguine

2 tablespoons margarine, butter or spread

3 cups sliced mushrooms (8 ounces)

1 cup chicken broth

1/4 cup crumbled blue cheese

1/4 teaspoon salt

1/3 cup water

1 tablespoon plus 2 teaspoons cornstarch

Melt 1 tablespoon margarine in 10-inch skillet over medium heat. Cook pork in margarine, turning once, until no longer pink in center. Remove pork from skillet; keep warm. Cook and drain linguine as directed on package.

Melt 2 tablespoons margarine in same skillet over medium heat. Cook mushrooms in margarine, stirring occasionally, until tender. Stir in broth, 2 tablespoons of the blue cheese and the salt; heat to boiling.

Mix water and cornstarch; stir into mushroom mixture. Heat to boiling, stirring constantly. Boil and stir 1 minute. Serve over pork and linguine. Sprinkle with remaining 2 tablespoons blue cheese.

1 Serving: Calories 385 (Calories from Fat 145); Fat 16g (Saturated 5g); Cholesterol 75mg; Sodium 600mg; Carbohydrate 29g (Dietary Fiber 1g); Protein 32g.

CURRIED CARIBBEAN PORK PASTA

4 SERVINGS

Like to make this dish extra special? Top it with chutney and raisins in addition to the coconut.

1 pound ground pork

1 clove garlic, finely chopped

1/2 cup mayonnaise or salad dressing

1/2 cup plain yogurt

1/4 cup frozen (thawed) orange juice concentrate

2 1/2 teaspoons curry powder

1 can (8 ounces) pineapple chunks in juice, drained, and 2 tablespoons juice reserved

1/4 cup sliced green onions (3 medium)

2 cups uncooked farfalle (bow tie) pasta (4 ounces)

1 small red bell pepper, cut into 1-inch pieces

1 can (11 ounces) mandarin orange segments, drained

1/4 cup coconut, toasted

Cook pork and garlic in 10-inch skillet over medium-high heat, stirring occasionally, until pork is no longer pink; drain. Stir in mayonnaise, yogurt, juice concentrate, curry powder and reserved pineapple juice. Fold in pineapple and onions. Cook until hot, stirring frequently.

Cook pasta as directed on package, adding bell pepper 4 minutes before pasta is done; drain. Toss pasta, bell peppers and pork mixture. Toss with orange segments. Sprinkle with coconut.

1 Serving: Calories 810 (Calories from Fat 370); Fat 41g (Saturated 11g); Cholesterol 90mg; Sodium 240mg; Carbohydrate 83g (Dietary Fiber 5g); Protein 32g.

ORZO- AND BACON- STUFFED TOMATOES

8 SERVINGS

A great recipe to use when garden tomatoes are abundant!

8 large tomatoes (about 3 inches in diameter)

1/2 pound bacon

1 medium onion, chopped (1/2 cup)

1 clove garlic, finely chopped

1 can (14 1/2 ounces) ready-to-serve chicken broth

1 cup uncooked rosamarina (orzo) pasta (6 ounces)

1 tablespoon chopped fresh or 1 teaspoon dried oregano leaves

1/8 teaspoon pepper

Cut thin slice from top of each tomato; set aside. Scoop out pulp from tomatoes, leaving 1/4-inch wall. Drain tomato pulp; chop and reserve 1 cup. Invert tomato shells onto paper towels to drain.

Heat oven to 400°. Grease jelly roll pan, 15 1/2 × 10 1/2 × 1 inch. Cook bacon in 10-inch skillet over medium-low heat, turning occasionally, until crisp. Drain bacon strips on paper towels. Drain drippings from skillet, reserving 1 tablespoon.

Heat reserved drippings in skillet over medium heat. Cook onion and garlic in drippings, stirring occasionally, until onion is tender. Stir in broth and pasta. Heat to boiling; reduce heat to low. Simmer uncovered about 15 minutes, stirring occasionally and scraping brown bits from bottom of skillet, until pasta is still slightly chewy. Crumble bacon into skillet; stir in reserved tomato pulp, the oregano and pepper.

Place tomato shells in jelly roll pan. Fill with pasta mixture; cover with reserved tomato tops. Bake about 20 minutes or until tomatoes are hot and tender but still hold their shape.

1 Serving: Calories 155 (Calories from Fat 45); Fat 5g (Saturated 2g); Cholesterol 5mg; Sodium 310mg; Carbohydrate 23g (Dietary Fiber 2g); Protein 7g.

CURRY SAUSAGE COUSCOUS

4 SERVINGS

1 pound bulk pork sausage

1 medium onion, chopped (1/2 cup)

1/2 teaspoon curry powder

1 clove garlic, finely chopped

2 1/4 cups chicken broth

1 tablespoon margarine, butter or spread

1 tablespoon chopped fresh parsley or 1 teaspoon dried parsley flakes

1/4 teaspoon salt

1 1/2 cups uncooked couscous

1/4 cup chopped peanuts

Cook sausage, onion, curry powder and garlic in 10-inch skillet over medium-high heat, stirring occasionally, until sausage is no longer pink; drain. Stir in broth, margarine, parsley and salt. Heat to boiling.

Stir in couscous; remove from heat. Cover and let stand about 5 minutes or until liquid is absorbed. Fluff with fork. Sprinkle with peanuts.

1 Serving: Calories 540 (Calories from Fat 225); Fat 25g (Saturated 7g); Cholesterol 45mg; Sodium 1300mg; Carbohydrate 59g (Dietary Fiber 4g); Protein 24g.

SPAGHETTI PIZZA

8 SERVINGS

1 package (7 ounces) spaghetti

1/2 pound bulk Italian sausage

2 eggs

3/4 cup shredded Parmesan cheese

1 1/2 teaspoons Italian seasoning

1 1/2 cups shredded mozzarella cheese
(6 ounces)

1 cup ricotta cheese

2 tablespoons milk

3/4 cup spaghetti sauce

1 small green bell pepper, coarsely
chopped (1/2 cup)

Heat oven to 350°. Grease cookie sheet or 12-inch pizza pan. Cook and drain spaghetti as directed on package. Cook sausage in 10-inch skillet over medium-high heat, stirring occasionally, until no longer pink; drain.

Beat eggs in large bowl with fork. Stir in 1/2 cup of the Parmesan cheese and the Italian seasoning. Mix together egg mixture and spaghetti. Spread in 11-inch circle on cookie sheet.

Mix 1 cup of the mozzarella cheese, the ricotta cheese and milk. Spread over spaghetti mixture to within 1 inch of edge. Spread with spaghetti sauce to within 1/4 inch of edge of ricotta mixture.

Top with sausage, bell pepper and the remaining Parmesan and mozzarella cheeses. Bake 25 to 30 minutes or until cheese begins to brown.

1 Serving: Calories 355 (Calories from Fat 160); Fat 18g (Saturated 8g); Cholesterol 100mg; Sodium 720mg; Carbohydrate 26g (Dietary Fiber 1g); Protein 23g.

SPICY PEANUT BUTTER-PORK PASTA

4 SERVINGS

1 1/2 cups uncooked rotini pasta (4 ounces)

1 tablespoon vegetable oil

1 pound pork tenderloin, cut into 1/2-inch
slices

1 medium onion, chopped (1/2 cup)

1 tablespoon finely chopped gingerroot

1 clove garlic, finely chopped

1/3 cup creamy peanut butter

1/4 cup chili sauce

1 teaspoon sesame oil

1/4 teaspoon salt

1/4 teaspoon ground red pepper (cayenne)

1 cup water

1/2 cup sliced green onions (5 medium)

4 roma (plum) tomatoes, chopped
(1 1/2 cups)

Cook and drain pasta as directed on package. Heat vegetable oil in 10-inch skillet over medium-high heat. Cook pork, onion, gingerroot and garlic in oil, stirring occasionally, until pork is no longer pink; reduce heat to low.

Stir in peanut butter, chili sauce, sesame oil, salt and red pepper. Gradually stir in water, stirring constantly, until peanut butter is melted. Heat to boiling; reduce heat to low. Simmer uncovered about 5 minutes, stirring frequently, until sauce is slightly thickened. Add pasta, green onions and tomatoes; toss until well coated.

1 Serving: Calories 455 (Calories from Fat 180); Fat 20g (Saturated 4g); Cholesterol 65mg; Sodium 470mg; Carbohydrate 38g (Dietary Fiber 3g); Protein 34g.

Spicy Peanut Butter-Pork Pasta

RIGATONI-SMOKED BRATWURST SKILLET

4 SERVINGS

A simple, weeknight main dish all done in one skillet! Toss a package of prewashed salad greens with your favorite dressing and some croutons, and dinner is served.

1 cup water

1 can (14 1/2 ounces) Italian-style stewed tomatoes, undrained

1 can (6 ounces) tomato paste

1 tablespoon sugar

1/2 teaspoon onion powder

1/4 teaspoon salt

1/8 teaspoon pepper

1 cup small curd creamed cottage cheese

2 cups uncooked rigatoni pasta (6 ounces)

1 pound smoked cooked bratwurst, kielbasa or ring bologna, sliced

2 tablespoons chopped fresh parsley

Mix water, tomatoes, tomato paste, sugar, onion powder, salt and pepper in 10-inch skillet; heat to boiling. Stir in cottage cheese; heat to boiling.

Stir in rigatoni and bratwurst. Heat to boiling; reduce heat to low. Cover and simmer 25 to 30 minutes, stirring frequently, until rigatoni is tender. Uncover and simmer about 5 minutes or until desired consistency. Stir in parsley.

1 Serving: Calories 725 (Calories from Fat 335); Fat 37g (Saturated 14g); Cholesterol 85mg; Sodium 1850mg; Carbohydrate 70g (Dietary Fiber 5g); Protein 33g.

SZECHUAN PORK

4 SERVINGS

1 pound pork tenderloin, cut into 1/4-inch slices

1 tablespoon soy sauce

2 teaspoons cornstarch

1/2 teaspoon ground red pepper (cayenne)

1 clove garlic, finely chopped

2 tablespoons vegetable oil

3 cups broccoli flowerets or 1 package (16 ounces) frozen broccoli cuts, thawed

2 small onions, cut into eighths

1 can (8 ounces) whole water chestnuts, drained

1/4 cup chicken broth

1/2 cup peanuts

4 cups hot cooked vermicelli

Mix pork, soy sauce, cornstarch, red pepper and garlic in glass or plastic bowl. Cover and refrigerate 20 minutes.

Heat wok or 12-inch skillet over high heat until hot. Add oil; rotate wok to coat side. Add pork; stir-fry until no longer pink. Add broccoli, onions and water chestnuts; stir-fry 2 minutes.

Stir in broth; heat to boiling. Stir in peanuts. Serve with vermicelli.

1 Serving: Calories 535 (Calories from Fat 190); Fat 21g (Saturated 4g); Cholesterol 70mg; Sodium 380mg; Carbohydrate 55g (Dietary Fiber 6g); Protein 38g.

ITALIAN SAUSAGE LASAGNA

8 SERVINGS

1 pound bulk Italian sausage

1 medium onion, chopped (1/2 cup)

1 clove garlic, crushed

2 tablespoons chopped fresh parsley

1 tablespoon chopped fresh or 1 teaspoon
    dried basil leaves

1 teaspoon sugar

1 can (16 ounces) whole tomatoes,
    undrained

1 can (15 ounces) tomato sauce

12 uncooked lasagna noodles (about
    12 ounces)

1 container (16 ounces) ricotta cheese or
    small curd creamed cottage cheese
    (2 cups)

1/2 cup grated Parmesan cheese

1 tablespoon chopped fresh parsley

1 tablespoon chopped fresh or
    1 1/2 teaspoons dried oregano leaves

2 cups shredded mozzarella cheese
    (8 ounces)

Cook sausage, onion and garlic in 10-inch skillet over medium-high heat, stirring occasionally, until sausage is no longer pink; drain. Stir in 2 tablespoons parsley, the basil, sugar, tomatoes and tomato sauce, breaking up tomatoes. Heat to boiling, stirring occasionally; reduce heat to low. Simmer uncovered about 45 minutes or until slightly thickened.

Heat oven to 350°. Cook and drain noodles as directed on package. Mix ricotta cheese, 1/4 cup of the Parmesan cheese, 1 tablespoon parsley and the oregano.

Spread 1 cup of the sauce in ungreased rectangular baking dish, 13 × 9 × 2 inches. Top with 4 noodles. Layer with 1 cup of the cheese mixture and 1 cup of the sauce. Sprinkle with 2/3 cup of the mozzarella cheese. Repeat with 4 noodles, the remaining cheese mixture, 1 cup of the sauce and 2/3 cup of the mozzarella cheese. Top with remaining noodles and sauce mixture. Sprinkle with remaining mozzarella and Parmesan cheeses.

Cover and bake 30 minutes. Uncover and bake 15 minutes longer or until hot and bubbly. Let stand 15 minutes before cutting.

1 Serving: Calories 505 (Calories from Fat 235); Fat 26g (Saturated 12g); Cholesterol 80mg; Sodium 1250mg; Carbohydrate 37g (Dietary Fiber 2g); Protein 33g.

TORTELLINI CORN CHOWDER

8 SERVINGS

1 tablespoon margarine, butter or spread

1 large onion, chopped (1 cup)

3 cups water

2 teaspoons chopped fresh or 1 teaspoon dried marjoram leaves

1/4 teaspoon coarsely ground pepper

1 package (9 ounces) refrigerated filled tortellini (any flavor)

2 medium potatoes, peeled and cut into 1/2-inch cubes

8 ounces lean prosciutto or fully cooked smoked ham, cut into 1/2-inch pieces (about 1 1/3 cups)

1 can (16 1/2 ounces) cream-style corn

1 can (11 ounces) whole kernel corn with red and green peppers, undrained

1 can (12 ounces) evaporated milk

Melt margarine in 4-quart saucepan over medium heat. Cook onion in margarine, stirring occasionally, until tender. Add water, marjoram and pepper; heat to boiling.

Add tortellini and potatoes. Heat to boiling; reduce heat to low. Cover and simmer about 15 minutes, stirring occasionally, until potatoes are tender. Stir in remaining ingredients. Heat to boiling; reduce heat to low. Simmer uncovered 5 minutes.

1 Serving: Calories 290 (Calories from Fat 100); Fat 11g (Saturated 4g); Cholesterol 55mg; Sodium 720mg; Carbohydrate 36g (Dietary Fiber 3g); Protein 15g.

STRAW AND HAY PASTA

4 SERVINGS

1 tablespoon margarine, butter or spread

1 1/2 cups sliced mushrooms (4 ounces)

4 ounces fully cooked smoked ham, cut into 1 × 1/4-inch strips

2 tablespoons chopped fresh parsley

2 tablespoons chopped onion

1/4 cup brandy or chicken broth

1 cup whipping (heavy) cream

1/4 teaspoon salt

1/4 teaspoon pepper

1 package (9 ounces) refrigerated fettuccine

1 package (9 ounces) refrigerated spinach fettuccine

1/2 cup shredded Parmesan cheese

Freshly ground pepper

Melt margarine in 10-inch skillet over medium-high heat. Cook mushrooms, ham, parsley and onion in margarine, stirring occasionally, until mushrooms are tender. Stir in brandy. Cook uncovered until liquid has evaporated.

Stir in whipping cream, salt and pepper. Heat to boiling; reduce heat to low. Simmer uncovered about 15 minutes, stirring frequently, until thickened.

Cook and drain fettuccines as directed on package. Mix fettuccines and sauce. Sprinkle with cheese. Serve with pepper.

1 Serving: Calories 715 (Calories from Fat 280); Fat 31g (Saturated 16g); Cholesterol 200mg; Sodium 740mg; Carbohydrate 87g (Dietary Fiber 6g); Protein 28g.

HARVEST TORTE

8 SERVINGS

When selecting butternut squash, look for ones that have hard, tough rinds and are heavy for their size.

Butternut Squash Sauce (right)

1 package (12 ounces) capellini (angel hair) pasta

2 cups diced fully cooked smoked ham (about 12 ounces)

1 1/2 cups mozzarella cheese (6 ounces)

3/4 cup dried cranberries

1/2 cup sliced green onions (5 medium)

1 tablespoon chopped fresh or 1 teaspoon dried rosemary leaves

2 eggs, slightly beaten

Heat oven to 375°. Grease springform pan, 10 × 3 inches; dust with flour. Prepare Butternut Squash Sauce. Cook and drain pasta as directed on package. Toss pasta, sauce and remaining ingredients. Spoon into pan.

Cover and bake 45 to 50 minutes or until hot. Cool uncovered in pan on wire rack 10 minutes; remove side of pan. Cut into wedges.

BUTTERNUT SQUASH SAUCE

1/2 butternut or buttercup squash (about 2 1/2 pounds), peeled and cut into 1-inch pieces (4 cups)

1 medium onion, coarsely chopped (1/2 cup)

2 cloves garlic

1 cup water

1 tablespoon margarine, butter or spread

1/2 teaspoon salt

1/4 teaspoon ground nutmeg

1/8 teaspoon pepper

1/2 cup milk

Mix all ingredients except milk in 3-quart saucepan. Heat to boiling; reduce heat to low. Cover and simmer about 20 minutes or until squash is tender.

Carefully spoon squash and cooking liquid into blender. Add milk. Cover and blend on until smooth.

1 Serving: Calories 370 (Calories from Fat 100); Fat 11g (Saturated 5g); Cholesterol 85mg; Sodium 820mg; Carbohydrate 50g (Dietary Fiber 5g); Protein 23g.

TUSCAN HAM, BEAN AND CABBAGE STEW

8 SERVINGS

1 tablespoon margarine, butter or spread

1 tablespoon olive or vegetable oil

8 ounces chopped fully cooked smoked ham (1 cup)

1 large onion, coarsely chopped (1 cup)

2 medium stalks celery, sliced (1 cup)

1 clove garlic, finely chopped

4 cups chicken broth

1 can (28 ounces) whole Italian-style tomatoes, undrained

3 cups uncooked radiatore (nugget) pasta (4 ounces)

2 cups coleslaw mix (4 ounces)

2 cans (15 to 16 ounces each) great northern beans, rinsed and drained

1 tablespoon chopped fresh or 1 teaspoon dried basil leaves

Heat margarine and oil in Dutch oven over medium heat. Cook ham, onion, celery and garlic in margarine mixture, stirring occasionally, until onion is tender. Stir in broth and tomatoes, breaking up tomatoes. Heat to boiling.

Stir in pasta. Heat to boiling; reduce heat to low. Cover and simmer about 10 minutes or until pasta is tender. Stir in remaining ingredients. Heat to boiling; reduce heat to low. Simmer uncovered about 3 minutes or until cabbage is tender.

1 Serving: Calories 275 (Calories from Fat 55); Fat 6g (Saturated 1g); Cholesterol 10mg; Sodium 1090mg; Carbohydrate 44g (Dietary Fiber 8g); Protein 19g.

GREEK LAMB AND ORZO

4 SERVINGS

1 pound ground lamb or beef

2 cans (16 ounces each) stewed tomatoes, undrained

1 medium stalk celery, cut into 1/2-inch pieces

1 cup uncooked rosamarina (orzo) pasta (3 ounces)

1/4 teaspoon salt

1/4 teaspoon ground red pepper (cayenne)

Plain yogurt, if desired

Cook lamb in 10-inch skillet over medium-high heat, stirring occasionally, until no longer pink; drain. Stir in tomatoes, celery, pasta, salt and red pepper. Heat to boiling; reduce heat to low.

Cover and simmer about 12 minutes, stirring frequently, until tomato liquid is absorbed and orzo is tender. Serve with yogurt.

1 Serving: Calories 375 (Calories from Fat 155); Fat 17g (Saturated 7g); Cholesterol 70mg; Sodium 560mg; Carbohydrate 35g (Dietary Fiber 3g); Protein 24g.

Greek Lamb and Orzo

JAZZING UP
SPAGHETTI SAUCE

Everybody seems to do it: They take a jar of their favorite spaghetti sauce and add a little of this and a little of that to make it special. We've listed 10 stir-in ideas below to help you jazz it up! Add any of the following stir-ins to a 14-ounce jar of your favorite spaghetti sauce and cook until hot.

1. Stir sauce into 1 pound cooked and crumbled ground beef, chicken, turkey or Italian sausage.

2. Stir in 2 cups fresh or thawed frozen vegetables such as roma (plum) tomatoes, sliced zucchini, sliced mushrooms, bell pepper strips or broccoli flowerets.

3. Stir in 1 tablespoon chopped fresh or 1 teaspoon dried herbs such as basil, Italian parsley, oregano or rosemary.

4. Stir in 1/2 cup finely shredded or grated Parmesan cheese and 1 clove garlic, finely chopped. The cheese will thicken the sauce.

5. Stir in 1 package (10 ounces) frozen chopped spinach, thawed and squeezed dry, 1/2 cup whipping (heavy) cream and 1/4 teaspoon ground nutmeg.

6. Stir in 1 can (15 to 16 ounces) cannellini beans, rinsed and drained, 1/4 teaspoon crushed red pepper flakes and 1 tablespoon chopped fresh parsley.

7. Stir in 1/3 cup crumbled feta cheese, 1/4 cup sliced ripe olives and 1 small zucchini, sliced.

8. Stir in 1 jar (6 ounces) marinated artichoke hearts, quartered.

9. Stir in 1 pound bacon, crisply cooked and crumbled; sprinkle servings with shredded Cheddar cheese.

10. Stir in 1 can (6 ounces) tuna, drained, 1/4 cup pimiento-stuffed olives, halved or sliced, and 2 tablespoons chopped parsley.

HUNGARIAN PORK GOULASH

8 SERVINGS

The Székely, who originated this interpretation of Hungarian goulash, come from the northern part of Hungary, once known as Transylvania and now a part of Romania. The Székely still live in their ancient homeland and claim to be direct descendants of Attila's Huns!

1 tablespoon vegetable oil

2 pounds pork boneless shoulder, cut into
    1-inch pieces

1 large onion, chopped (1 cup)

1 clove garlic, chopped

3 cups water

2 tablespoons paprika

2 teaspoons chicken bouillon granules

1 teaspoon caraway seed

1 teaspoon salt

1/8 teaspoon pepper

2 cans (16 ounces each) sauerkraut,
    drained

1/4 cup cold water

2 tablespoons all-purpose flour

1 cup sour cream

8 cups hot cooked egg noodles

Chopped fresh parsley, if desired

Heat oil in Dutch oven or 12-inch skillet over medium heat. Cook pork, onion and garlic in oil, stirring occasionally, until pork is no longer pink; drain. Stir in 3 cups water, the paprika, bouillon granules, caraway seed, salt and pepper. Heat to boiling; reduce heat to low. Cover and simmer 1 hour, stirring occasionally.

Stir in sauerkraut. Heat to boiling; reduce heat to low. Cover and simmer about 30 minutes, stirring occasionally, until pork is tender.

Shake 1/4 cup water and the flour in tightly covered container; stir into pork mixture. Heat to boiling, stirring constantly. Boil and stir 1 minute; reduce heat to low. Stir in sour cream; heat just until hot. Serve over noodles. Sprinkle with parsley.

1 Serving: Calories 485 (Calories from Fat 205); Fat 23g (Saturated 9g); Cholesterol 130mg; Sodium 1350mg; Carbohydrate 50g (Dietary Fiber 7g); Protein 26g.

4

POULTRY AND SEAFOOD

String Pie (p.114),
Pesto Parmesan
Loaf (p.176)

TURKEY TACO SHELLS

6 SERVINGS

Great taco flavor in a pasta shell!

12 uncooked jumbo pasta shells

1 pound lean ground turkey

1 medium onion, chopped (1/2 cup)

1 1/2 teaspoons chili powder

1 package (3 ounces) cream cheese, softened

3/4 cup taco sauce

1 cup shredded Colby-Monterey Jack cheese (4 ounces)

1/2 cup crushed corn chips

1/2 cup sour cream

1/3 cup sliced green onions (4 medium)

Heat oven to 350°. Grease rectangular baking dish, 12 × 8 × 2 inches. Cook and drain pasta as directed on package.

Cook turkey and onion in 10-inch skillet over medium-high heat 5 to 6 minutes, stirring occasionally, until turkey is no longer pink; reduce heat to medium-low. Stir in chili powder, cream cheese and 1/4 cup of the taco sauce. Cook 2 to 3 minutes, stirring occasionally, until cheese melts.

Fill pasta shells with turkey mixture. Place in baking dish. Pour remaining taco sauce over shells. Cover and bake 20 minutes. Sprinkle with cheese and corn chips. Bake uncovered about 10 minutes longer or until cheese is melted. Garnish with sour cream and green onions.

1 Serving: Calories 385 (Calories from Fat 215); Fat 24g (Saturated 12g); Cholesterol 100mg; Sodium 440mg; Carbohydrate 20g (Dietary Fiber 2g); Protein 24g.

CREAMY CHICKEN AND RIGATONI

8 SERVINGS

1 tablespoon olive or vegetable oil

1 pound boneless, skinless chicken breast halves, cut into 1-inch pieces

2 cloves garlic, finely chopped

2 teaspoons dried basil leaves

2 teaspoons dried oregano leaves

2 cans (14 1/2 ounces each) diced tomatoes, well drained

2 cups whipping (heavy) cream

1/2 teaspoon salt

1/2 teaspoon freshly ground pepper

1/4 teaspoon ground red pepper (cayenne)

1 package (16 ounces) rigatoni pasta

1 package (16 ounces) frozen broccoli, red pepper, onions and mushrooms, thawed and drained

Shredded Parmesan cheese, if desired

Heat oil in Dutch oven over medium-high heat. Cook chicken, garlic, basil and oregano in oil about 5 minutes, stirring frequently, until chicken is no longer pink in center.

Stir in tomatoes, whipping cream, salt, pepper and red pepper. Heat to boiling; reduce heat to low. Simmer uncovered about 10 minutes or until slightly thickened.

Cook and drain rigatoni as directed on package. Stir rigatoni and vegetables into chicken mixture; cook until hot. Serve with cheese.

1 Serving: Calories 495 (Calories from Fat 205); Fat 23g (Saturated 12g); Cholesterol 95mg; Sodium 370mg; Carbohydrate 54g (Dietary Fiber 4g); Protein 22g.

CHICKEN SPAGHETTI OLÉ

6 SERVINGS

This is a wonderful way to use leftover chicken or turkey.

6 ounces uncooked spaghetti

1 tablespoon margarine, butter or spread

1 small green bell pepper, chopped (1/2 cup)

1 medium stalk celery, chopped (1/2 cup)

1 small onion, chopped (1/4 cup)

1 can (10 ounces) whole tomatoes and green chilies, undrained

1 can (8 ounces) tomato sauce

1 package (8 ounces) process cheese spread loaf

1/2 teaspoon salt

1/4 teaspoon pepper

2 cups diced cooked chicken or turkey

Heat oven to 350°. Grease rectangular baking dish, 12 × 8 × 2 inches. Cook and drain spaghetti as directed on package.

Melt margarine in 12-inch skillet over medium heat. Cook bell pepper, celery and onion in margarine, stirring occasionally, until tender. Stir in tomatoes and green chilies, tomato sauce, cheese, salt and pepper; reduce heat to low. Simmer uncovered, stirring frequently, until cheese is melted.

Stir in chicken and spaghetti. Spoon into baking dish. Bake uncovered about 30 minutes or until bubbly around edges.

1 Serving: Calories 375 (Calories from Fat 155); Fat 17g (Saturated 9g); Cholesterol 75mg; Sodium 1090mg; Carbohydrate 30g (Dietary Fiber 2g); Protein 27g.

CREAMY CHICKEN AND FUSILLI

5 SERVINGS

1 1/2 cups uncooked fusilli pasta (4 1/2 ounces)

1 tablespoon margarine, butter or spread

1 pound boneless, skinless chicken breast halves, cut into 1-inch pieces

1 small red onion, sliced

1 clove garlic, finely chopped

1 medium yellow bell pepper, cut into strips

1 1/2 cups frozen green peas

2 packages (3 ounces each) cream cheese, softened

1/2 cup chicken broth

2 tablespoons dry white wine (or nonalcoholic) or apple juice

2 tablespoons chopped fresh or 2 teaspoons dried basil leaves

1/2 teaspoon salt

1/4 teaspoon pepper

Cook and drain pasta as directed on package. Melt margarine in 12-inch skillet over medium-high heat. Cook chicken, onion and garlic in margarine 3 to 4 minutes, stirring occasionally, until chicken is light brown. Stir in bell pepper and peas. Cook, stirring occasionally, until vegetables are crisp-tender.

Mix cream cheese, broth, wine, basil, salt and pepper. Stir into chicken mixture. Cook, stirring constantly, until cream cheese is melted. Toss with pasta.

1 Serving: Calories 410 (Calories from Fat 160); Fat 18g (Saturated 9g); Cholesterol 85mg; Sodium 500mg; Carbohydrate 36g (Dietary Fiber 3g); Protein 29g.

CHICKEN ROTINI WITH RED PEPPER

5 SERVINGS

The toasted pine nuts add an interesting nutty texture and flavor to this dish.

4 cups uncooked tricolor or spinach rotini pasta (10 ounces)

1/4 cup pine nuts or chopped almonds

2 tablespoons margarine, butter or spread

1 pound boneless, skinless chicken breast halves, cut into 1/2-inch slices

3 cloves garlic, finely chopped

1 can (10 1/2 ounces) condensed chicken broth

1 can (5 ounces) evaporated milk

2 tablespoons all-purpose flour

1/2 teaspoon salt

1/4 teaspoon pepper

1/2 cup roasted red bell peppers (from 7-ounce jar), drained and sliced

3 tablespoons grated Parmesan cheese

2 tablespoons chopped fresh chives

Cook and drain pasta as directed on package. Heat 10-inch skillet over medium-high heat. Cook pine nuts in skillet 1 to 2 minutes, stirring frequently, until light brown. Remove pine nuts from skillet.

Melt margarine in same skillet over medium-high heat. Cook chicken and garlic in margarine 3 to 4 minutes, stirring occasionally, until chicken is light brown.

Shake broth, milk, flour, salt and pepper in tightly covered container. Gradually stir into chicken mixture. Heat to boiling, stirring constantly. Boil and stir 1 minute. Stir in bell peppers, cheese, chives and pine nuts. Toss with pasta. Sprinkle with additional chopped fresh chives if desired.

1 Serving: Calories 625 (Calories from Fat 170); Fat 19g (Saturated 5g); Cholesterol 155mg; Sodium 800mg; Carbohydrate 79g (Dietary Fiber 6g); Protein 40g.

PARMESAN AND ROMANO CHEESES

Romano cheese is usually made from sheep's milk, not cow's milk, as is Parmesan. Some Romano cheese made in the United States, however, may be made with cow's milk or a combination of sheep and cow's milk. Romano has a drier, sharper flavor than Parmesan, and is well suited for pastas served with cured meats such as ham, bacon or prosciutto. Both Romano and Parmesan cheeses add wonderful flavor to pasta, and are at their very best when freshly grated. These cheeses are available fresh sold either in wedges or preshredded form or are available in the dry, grated form sold in the familiar shaker canisters.

FARFALLE WITH CILANTRO PESTO

4 SERVINGS

3 cups uncooked farfalle (bow tie) pasta (6 ounces)

2 tablespoons olive or vegetable oil

3 tablespoons plain yogurt

2 teaspoons lime juice

1/4 cup grated Parmesan cheese

1 tablespoon slivered almonds, toasted

2 cloves garlic

1/8 teaspoon pepper

1 cup firmly packed fresh cilantro

2 teaspoons olive or vegetable oil

1 1/2 cups cut-up cooked chicken or turkey (about 8 ounces)

2 medium yellow summer squash or zucchini, cubed (about 3 cups)

8 cherry tomatoes, cut into fourths

Cook and drain pasta as directed on package. Place 2 tablespoons oil, the yogurt, lime juice, cheese, almonds, garlic, pepper and cilantro in blender. Cover and blend on medium speed about 2 minutes, stopping blender occasionally to scrape sides, until almost smooth.

Heat 2 teaspoons oil in 10-inch skillet over medium heat. Cook chicken and squash in oil, stirring occasionally, until squash is crisp-tender. Stir in cilantro mixture, pasta and tomatoes; cook until hot.

1 Serving: Calories 395 (Calories from Fat 145); Fat 16g (Saturated 4g); Cholesterol 50mg; Sodium 170mg; Carbohydrate 40g (Dietary Fiber 3g); Protein 26g.

CHICKEN TORTELLINI IN MUSHROOM SAUCE

6 SERVINGS

To make this a quick-to-fix recipe, substitute a pouch of sauce mix for the "scratch" Béchamel Sauce. Make sure the pouch makes two cups of sauce.

2 cups Béchamel Sauce (page 143)

2 packages (9 ounces each) refrigerated chicken-filled tortellini

1 tablespoon margarine, butter or spread

3 cups chopped portobello or shiitake mushrooms (about 6 ounces)

2 teaspoons chopped fresh or 3/4 teaspoon dried sage leaves

Prepare Béchamel Sauce as directed—except double ingredients to yield 2 cups sauce. Cook and drain tortellini as directed on package.

Melt margarine in 10-inch skillet over medium heat. Cook mushrooms in margarine, stirring occasionally, until brown and tender. Stir mushrooms and sage into Béchamel Sauce. Toss with pasta.

1 Serving: Calories 275 (Calories from Fat 100); Fat 11g (Saturated 3g); Cholesterol 75mg; Sodium 660mg; Carbohydrate 29g (Dietary Fiber 1g); Protein 16g.

Santa Fe Chicken-Tortellini Casserole

6 SERVINGS

Serve this zesty casserole with salsa and sour cream for real southwestern flavor.

1 package (9 ounces) refrigerated cheese-filled tortellini

3 tablespoons olive or vegetable oil

2 cups broccoli flowerets

1 medium onion, chopped (1/2 cup)

1 medium red bell pepper, chopped (1 cup)

3 tablespoons all-purpose flour

3/4 cup milk

3/4 cup chicken broth

1 teaspoon ground cumin

4 cups cut-up cooked chicken

3/4 cup shredded Monterey Jack cheese (3 ounces)

1/2 cup shredded Colby cheese (2 ounces)

1/2 cup crushed tortilla chips

Cook and drain tortellini as directed on package. Heat oven to 325°. Grease 3-quart casserole. Heat 1 tablespoon of the oil in 10-inch skillet over medium-high heat. Cook broccoli, onion and bell pepper in oil about 3 minutes, stirring frequently, until crisp-tender. Remove broccoli mixture from skillet.

Cook flour and remaining 2 tablespoons oil in same skillet over low heat, stirring constantly, until smooth. Stir in milk, broth and cumin. Heat to boiling over medium heat, stirring constantly; remove from heat. Stir in chicken, Monterey Jack cheese, the tortellini and broccoli mixture. Spoon into casserole.

Santa Fe Chicken-Tortellini Casserole

Bake uncovered 25 to 35 minutes or until bubbly. During last several minutes of baking, sprinkle with Colby cheese and tortilla chips; bake until cheese is melted.

1 Serving: Calories 470 (Calories from Fat 225); Fat 25g (Saturated 9g); Cholesterol 145mg; Sodium 570mg; Carbohydrate 20g (Dietary Fiber 2g); Protein 43g.

Chicken Tetrazzini

6 SERVINGS

1 package (7 ounces) spaghetti, broken in half

1/4 cup margarine, butter or spread

1/4 cup all-purpose flour

1/2 teaspoon salt

1/4 teaspoon pepper

1 cup chicken broth

1 cup whipping (heavy) cream

2 tablespoons dry sherry or chicken broth

2 cups cubed cooked chicken

1 can (4 ounces) sliced mushrooms, drained

1/2 cup grated Parmesan cheese

Heat oven to 350°. Grease 2-quart casserole. Cook and drain spaghetti as directed on package. Melt margarine in 3-quart saucepan over low heat. Stir in flour, salt and pepper. Cook, stirring constantly, until smooth and bubbly; remove from heat. Stir in broth and whipping cream. Heat to boiling, stirring constantly. Boil and stir 1 minute. Stir in sherry, spaghetti, chicken and mushrooms.

Spoon into casserole. Sprinkle with cheese. Bake uncovered about 30 minutes or until bubbly in center.

1 Serving: Calories 520 (Calories from Fat 295); Fat 33g (Saturated 13g); Cholesterol 90mg; Sodium 740mg; Carbohydrate 34g (Dietary Fiber 1g); Protein 23g.

TURKEY–POPPY SEED CASSEROLE

8 SERVINGS

This is a great dish to take to a potluck supper!

4 cups uncooked egg noodles (8 ounces)

1 tablespoon margarine, butter or spread

1 pound ground turkey

1 medium onion, chopped (1/2 cup)

1 small green bell pepper, chopped (1/2 cup)

1 can (14 1/2 ounces) diced tomatoes, undrained

1/2 teaspoon salt

1/2 teaspoon pepper

1 1/2 cups small curd creamed cottage cheese

1 cup plain yogurt

2 tablespoons poppy seed

2 tablespoons grated Romano cheese

Heat oven to 375°. Grease 2-quart casserole. Cook and drain noodles as directed on package.

Melt margarine in 10-inch skillet over medium heat. Cook turkey, onion and bell pepper in margarine 4 to 6 minutes, stirring frequently, until turkey is no longer pink. Stir in tomatoes, salt and pepper.

Mix cottage cheese, yogurt and poppy seed in large bowl. Stir in noodles. Spoon three-fourths of noodle mixture into casserole. Spoon turkey mixture over noodles. Top with remaining noodles.

Cover and bake 40 minutes. Sprinkle with cheese. Uncover and bake 5 to 10 minutes longer or until hot and bubbly. Let stand 10 minutes before serving.

1 Serving: Calories 295 (Calories from Fat 110); Fat 12g (Saturated 4g); Cholesterol 70mg; Sodium 480mg; Carbohydrate 26g (Dietary Fiber 2g); Protein 23g.

CURRIED TURKEY SPAGHETTI

4 SERVINGS

1/2 pound ground turkey or beef

1 medium onion, chopped (1/2 cup)

1 clove garlic, finely chopped

3/4 cup chopped unpeeled tart eating apple (1 medium)

1/4 cup chopped fresh parsley

1/4 cup apple juice

1 1/2 teaspoons curry powder

1/2 teaspoon ground cumin

1/8 teaspoon ground red pepper (cayenne)

1 can (16 ounces) whole tomatoes, undrained

6 ounces uncooked spaghetti

2 tablespoons chopped peanuts, if desired

Cook turkey, onion and garlic in 10-inch skillet over medium heat, stirring occasionally, until turkey is no longer pink; drain. Stir in remaining ingredients except spaghetti and peanuts, breaking up tomatoes. Heat to boiling; reduce heat to low. Simmer uncovered about 5 minutes, stirring occasionally, until apple is tender.

Cook and drain spaghetti as directed on package. Serve sauce over spaghetti. Sprinkle with peanuts.

1 Serving: Calories 320 (Calories from Fat 65); Fat 7g (Saturated 2g); Cholesterol 40mg; Sodium 230mg; Carbohydrate 49g (Dietary Fiber 4g); Protein 19g.

ℛOASTED 𝒢ARLIC

2 TO **8** SERVINGS

Roasted garlic is absolutely delicious! Roasting creates a mellow, mild flavor that's wonderful on French bread, in mashed or baked potatoes, or added to melted butter for vegetables or in dips.

Garlic belongs to the lily family and is related to onions, chives, leeks and shallots. The garlic bulb is made up of as many as fifteen sections called cloves, each of which is covered with a thin, papery skin. There are four types of garlic available: American, Italian and Mexican. Italian and Mexican garlic have a pink-mauve colored outer skin and are slightly milder than American garlic. Another type is called elephant garlic. Elephant garlic is the size of small grapefruit, so it is the "elephant" of garlic. Each huge clove weighs an average of one ounce. This type of garlic has the mildest flavor.

Purchase garlic bulbs that are firm and plump, avoiding those that are soft, shriveled or stored in the refrigerated section of the produce area. Garlic should be stored in an open container in a cool, dry location.

1 to 4 bulbs garlic

1 teaspoon olive or vegetable oil for each bulb garlic

Salt and pepper

French bread slices, if desired

Heat oven to 350°. Carefully peel away paper skin around bulb, leaving just enough to hold garlic together. Trim top of garlic bulb about 1/2 inch to expose cloves. Place stem end down on 12-inch square of aluminum foil. Drizzle each bulb with 1 teaspoon oil and sprinkle with salt and pepper. Wrap securely in foil and place in pie plate or shallow baking pan.

Bake 45 to 50 minutes or until garlic is very tender when pierced with toothpick or fork. Cool slightly. To serve, gently squeeze garlic out of cloves and spread on bread.

PASTA SHELLS WITH CHICKEN AND BROCCOLI

6 SERVINGS

2 tablespoons vegetable oil

1 cup chopped broccoli

1/3 cup chopped onion

2 cloves garlic, finely chopped

1 medium carrot, cut into julienne strips

2 cups cut-up cooked chicken or turkey

1 teaspoon salt

2 medium tomatoes, chopped (1 1/2 cups)

4 cups hot cooked medium pasta shells

1/3 cup grated Parmesan cheese

2 tablespoons chopped fresh parsley

Heat oil in 10-inch skillet over medium heat. Cook broccoli, onion, garlic and carrot in oil about 10 minutes, stirring occasionally, until broccoli is crisp-tender.

Stir in chicken, salt and tomatoes. Cook about 3 minutes, stirring occasionally, just until chicken is hot. Toss with pasta. Sprinkle with cheese and parsley.

1 Serving: Calories 295 (Calories from Fat 90); Fat 10g (Saturated 3g); Cholesterol 45mg; Sodium 490mg; Carbohydrate 32g (Dietary Fiber 2g); Protein 21g.

CHICKEN WITH LEMON-CHIVE PASTA AND PEPPERS

4 SERVINGS

1/4 cup olive or vegetable oil

4 skinless, boneless chicken breasts (about 1 pound)

1 small red bell pepper, diced

1 cup frozen peas, thawed

1 teaspoon grated lemon peel

1 tablespoon chopped fresh chives

1/2 teaspoon salt

1/8 teaspoon pepper

Dash of ground nutmeg

2 tablespoons lemon juice

4 cups hot cooked pasta (any variety)

Freshly ground pepper, if desired

Heat oil in 10-inch skillet over medium-high heat. Cook chicken in oil about 15 to 20 minutes, turning once, until juice is no longer pink when centers of thickest pieces are cut. Remove from skillet; keep warm. In same skillet, cook bell pepper, peas, lemon peel, chives, salt, pepper and nutmeg, stirring occasionally, until bell peppers are crisp-tender. Stir in lemon juice; cook until hot. Toss pasta with vegetable mixture. Serve chicken over pasta; sprinkle with freshly ground pepper.

1 Serving: Calories 470 (Calories from Fat 160); Fat 18g (Saturated 3g); Cholesterol 65mg; Sodium 360mg; Carbohydrate 46g (Dietary Fiber 3g); Protein 34g.

Chicken with Lemon-Chive Pasta and Peppers

HOMEMADE "SUN-DRIED" TOMATOES

Sun-dried tomatoes add instant flavor pizzazz to so many foods. These dried morsels have an intense flavor, retain their sweetness and have a chewy texture. Red plum tomatoes are most often used for drying but you may also be able to find dried yellow tomatoes. Most "sun-dried" tomatoes available commercially are not actually dried in the sun because of the difficulty of achieving the necessary sunlight, temperature and humidity conditions needed for successful results. Instead, dried tomatoes available in grocery stores have been mechanically dried indoors. Two types of sun-dried tomatoes can be found in the store: oil-packed dried tomatoes or those packed loose and dry in cellophane packages. Sun-dried tomatoes can sometimes be expensive to buy, but are very easily and inexpensively made at home in your oven with the same delicious results!

1. Select bright red, ripe plum (also known as *roma* or Italian) tomatoes. This variety of tomato works best for drying because it is thick-fleshed and has few seeds. Regular tomatoes can be used, but will take longer to dry because they contain more liquid and seed. If you use regular tomatoes, select small-sized ones.

2. Rinse tomatoes under cold water and remove stems; drain on paper towels.

3. Cut plum tomatoes lengthwise in half (*cut regular tomatoes into quarters, this will help to speed drying*); scoop out seeds with small spoon.

4. Heat oven to 200°. Place broiler rack in broiler pan. Place tomato halves, in a single layer, cut sides down on broiler rack. Place larger tomatoes on outer edges of rack for more even cooking.*

5. Dry in oven for 6 to 12 hours or until tomatoes are shriveled, dry to the touch and very chewy in texture, turning once after 4 hours. The edges may be crisp, but tomatoes should not be crisp in the center; they will be somewhat pliable. Check after 6 hours and remove any smaller tomatoes that have dried. Tomatoes will be dark red in color and some pieces may have brown or dark spots. Tomatoes may darken during storage but they are still safe to eat.

6. Remove tomatoes from the oven and cool completely. Store dry and loosely packed in tightly covered containers in a cool, dark location for up to 6 months. **For food safety reasons, tomatoes dried at home cannot be stored in oil. There is a remote possibility that botulinal spores could form into deadly toxins due to the low-oxygen condition created by storing in oil.** (Commercially available dried tomatoes packed in oil are safe to eat, however, due to the way in which they are manufactured.)

7. Tomatoes need to be rehydrated before using. To rehydrate dried tomatoes, place tomatoes in small bowl and cover with hot or boiling water. Allow to stand 15 to 30 minutes or until softened.

Note: If using a food dehydrator, follow manufacturer's directions for drying tomatoes.

The recipes in this book that use sun-dried tomatoes are Roasted Red Bell Pepper Pasta (page 21), Pasta Torte Slices (page 42), Fettuccine with Chicken and Sun-dried Tomato Sauce (page 110), Mostaccioli with Sun-dried Tomato Pesto (page 130), Farfalle with Mushroom-Cilantro Sauce (page 136), Rigatoni with Artichokes (page 148), Pesto Parmesan Loaf (page 176), and Italian Tuna Pasta Salad (page 170).

CHICKEN WITH APRICOT CREAM SAUCE

4 SERVINGS

3 cups uncooked radiatore (nugget) pasta (9 ounces)

2 tablespoons margarine, butter or spread

1 pound boneless, skinless chicken breast halves, cut into 1-inch pieces

1/4 cup sliced green onions (3 medium)

1 can (12 ounces) evaporated milk

2 tablespoons all-purpose flour

1/2 teaspoon salt

1/4 teaspoon pepper

1 can (16 ounces) apricot halves, drained and cut into fourths

2 tablespoons sliced almonds, toasted

Cook and drain pasta as directed on package. Melt margarine in 10-inch skillet over medium heat. Cook chicken and onions in margarine 3 to 5 minutes, stirring occasionally, until chicken is light brown.

Shake milk, flour, salt and pepper in tightly covered container. Gradually stir into chicken mixture. Heat to boiling, stirring constantly. Boil and stir 1 minute. Stir in apricots. Pour sauce over pasta. Sprinkle with almonds.

1 Serving: Calories 615 (Calories from Fat 170); Fat 19g (Saturated 6g); Cholesterol 85mg; Sodium 480mg; Carbohydrate 77g (Dietary Fiber 4g); Protein 38g.

CHICKEN-ARTICHOKE TOSS

6 SERVINGS

3 cups uncooked radiatore (nugget) pasta (9 ounces)

1 jar (6 ounces) marinated artichoke hearts, undrained

1 pound boneless, skinless chicken breast halves, cut into 1/2-inch slices

3 cups sliced mushrooms (8 ounces)

1 jar (7 ounces) roasted red peppers, sliced

3/4 cup chicken broth

1/2 cup dry white wine (or nonalcoholic) or apple juice

1 tablespoon cornstarch

1/2 teaspoon salt

1/4 teaspoon pepper

1 tablespoon chopped fresh parsley

Cook and drain pasta as directed on package. Drain liquid from artichokes into 10-inch skillet; heat over medium-high heat. Cook chicken in liquid 3 minutes, stirring occasionally. Stir in mushrooms. Cook 4 to 6 minutes, stirring occasionally until chicken is light brown and no longer pink. Stir in artichokes and peppers.

Shake broth, wine, cornstarch, salt and pepper in tightly covered container. Gradually stir into chicken mixture. Heat to boiling, stirring constantly. Boil and stir 1 minute. Toss with pasta. Sprinkle with parsley.

1 Serving: Calories 370 (Calories from Fat 35); Fat 4g (Saturated 1g); Cholesterol 40mg; Sodium 400mg; Carbohydrate 59g (Dietary Fiber 3g); Protein 27g.

SPAGHETTI WITH BACON AND CHICKEN LIVERS

4 SERVINGS

8 ounces uncooked spaghetti

1 tablespoon margarine, butter or spread

8 ounces chicken livers, cut into fourths

4 slices bacon, cut into 1/2-inch pieces

1 jar (14 ounces) chunky-style spaghetti sauce

2 tablespoons vermouth, dry white wine or nonalcoholic wine

2 hard-cooked eggs, chopped

Chopped fresh parsley, if desired

Cook and drain spaghetti as directed on package. Melt margarine in 2-quart saucepan over medium heat. Cook chicken livers and bacon in margarine 4 to 6 minutes, stirring occasionally, until livers are brown and bacon is partially crisp; drain.

Stir in spaghetti sauce and vermouth. Simmer uncovered 5 minutes, stirring occasionally. Place spaghetti on serving platter. Pour sauce over spaghetti. Sprinkle with eggs and parsley.

1 Serving: Calories 450 (Calories from Fat 145); Fat 16g (Saturated 4g); Cholesterol 335mg; Sodium 960mg; Carbohydrate 57g (Dietary Fiber 4g); Protein 23g.

TARRAGON CHICKEN LASAGNA

6 SERVINGS

6 uncooked lasagna noodles

1 tablespoon margarine, butter or spread

1 1/2 cups sliced mushrooms (4 ounces)

1 medium onion, chopped (1/2 cup)

1 cup chicken broth

2 tablespoons chopped fresh or 1 teaspoon dried tarragon leaves

1/4 teaspoon salt

1/4 teaspoon pepper

1 package (8 ounces) cream cheese, softened

1 cup shredded Swiss cheese (4 ounces)

1 1/2 cups cooked diced chicken or turkey

1 jar (2 ounces) diced pimientos, drained

Heat oven to 325°. Grease rectangular baking dish, 12 × 8 × 2 inches. Cook and drain noodles as directed on package.

Melt margarine in 12-inch skillet over medium heat. Cook mushrooms and onion in margarine, stirring occasionally, until tender. Stir in broth, 1 tablespoon of the tarragon, the salt and pepper. Heat to boiling; reduce heat to low. Stir in cream cheese and Swiss cheese until melted. Stir in chicken and pimientos.

Cut noodles crosswise in half. Arrange 6 pieces, overlapping edges, in baking dish. Spread half of the sauce over noodles. Repeat layers of noodles and sauce. Cover and bake 25 to 30 minutes or until bubbly around edges. Sprinkle with remaining 1 tablespoon tarragon.

1 Serving: Calories 370 (Calories from Fat 205); Fat 23g (Saturated 13g); Cholesterol 85mg; Sodium 430mg; Carbohydrate 20g (Dietary Fiber 1g); Protein 22g.

SPINACH-STUFFED CHICKEN ROLLS

6 SERVINGS

These pretty chicken rolls are a great company dish.

1 package (9 ounces) refrigerated spinach
   fettuccine

6 boneless, skinless chicken breast halves
   (about 1 1/2 pounds)

1 package (10 ounces) frozen chopped
   spinach, thawed and squeezed to drain

1/2 cup ricotta cheese

2 tablespoons grated Parmesan cheese

1/2 teaspoon pepper

1/4 teaspoon salt

1 tablespoon vegetable oil

1 jar (26 to 28 ounces) spaghetti sauce

1/4 cup shredded mozzarella cheese
   (1 ounce)

Cook and drain fettuccine as directed on package. Flatten chicken breast halves to 1/4-inch thickness between plastic wrap or waxed paper. Mix spinach, ricotta cheese, Parmesan cheese, pepper and salt. Spread about 1/4 cup spinach mixture on each chicken breast half; roll up and secure with toothpicks.

Heat oil in 10-inch skillet over medium-high heat. Cook chicken rolls in oil 4 to 5 minutes, turning frequently, until brown on all sides. Pour spaghetti sauce over chicken rolls; reduce heat to low. Cover and simmer 20 minutes. Serve chicken rolls and sauce over fettuccine. Sprinkle with mozzarella cheese.

1 Serving: Calories 440 (Calories from Fat 135); Fat 15g (Saturated 4g); Cholesterol 115mg; Sodium 1100mg; Carbohydrate 42g (Dietary Fiber 4g); Protein 38g.

CHICKEN CACCIATORE

4 SERVINGS

1 tablespoon olive or vegetable oil

1 pound boneless, skinless chicken breasts,
   cut into 1-inch pieces

1 cup sliced mushrooms (3 ounces)

1 medium green bell pepper, chopped
   (1 cup)

2 tablespoons finely chopped onion

2 cloves garlic, finely chopped

1/2 cup dry white wine (or nonalcoholic) or
   chicken broth

1 teaspoon red or white wine vinegar

1 jar (14 ounces) spaghetti sauce

4 cups hot cooked spaghetti

Heat oil in 10-inch skillet over medium-high heat. Cook chicken in oil, stirring occasionally, until brown. Stir in mushrooms, bell pepper, onion and garlic. Cook 6 to 8 minutes, stirring occasionally, until bell pepper and onion are crisp-tender and chicken is no longer pink in center.

Stir in wine and vinegar. Cook 3 minutes. Stir in spaghetti sauce. Simmer uncovered 10 to 12 minutes to blend flavors. Serve over spaghetti.

1 Serving: Calories 460 (Calories from Fat 110); Fat 12g (Saturated 2g); Cholesterol 65mg; Sodium 740mg; Carbohydrate 52g (Dietary Fiber 3g); Protein 35g.

THAI CHICKEN WITH CELLOPHANE NOODLES

4 SERVINGS

1 package (3 3/4 ounces) cellophane noodles (bean threads)

2 tablespoons vegetable oil

1 pound boneless, skinless chicken breast halves or thighs, cut into thin slices

2 medium carrots, thinly sliced (1 cup)

4 serrano or jalapeño chilies, seeded and finely chopped

2 cups shredded napa (Chinese) cabbage (8 ounces)

2 medium stalks celery, sliced diagonally (1 cup)

3 green onions, cut into 2-inch pieces

1/3 cup fish sauce or soy sauce

2 teaspoons grated lime peel

Cover noodles with cold water. Let stand 20 minutes; drain. Cut into 3- to 4-inch pieces.

Heat wok or 12-inch skillet over high heat until hot. Add oil; rotate wok to coat side. Add chicken, carrots and chilies; stir-fry about 4 minutes or until chicken is no longer pink in center. Remove chicken mixture from wok.

Add cabbage, celery and onions to wok; stir-fry 1 minute. Add chicken mixture, noodles, fish sauce and lime peel; cook and stir about 1 minute or until hot.

1 Serving: Calories 295 (Calories from Fat 90); Fat 10g (Saturated 2g); Cholesterol 60mg; Sodium 1480mg; Carbohydrate 27g (Dietary Fiber 3g); Protein 27g.

ITALIAN CHICKEN SKILLET

4 SERVINGS

1 tablespoon olive or vegetable oil

4 boneless, skinless chicken breast halves, (about 1 pound)

2 cloves garlic, finely chopped

2 large bell peppers, cut into 1-inch squares

1 medium onion, thinly sliced

2 medium zucchini, sliced

1/4 cup 1/4-inch strips sliced pepperoni (about 1 ounce)

1/4 cup chicken broth or dry red wine (or nonalcoholic)

1 1/2 teaspoons chopped fresh or 1/4 teaspoon dried thyme leaves

1 1/2 teaspoons chopped fresh or 1/4 teaspoon dried rosemary leaves

1/4 teaspoon salt

1/8 teaspoon pepper

4 cups hot cooked fettuccine, linguine or vermicelli

1 tablespoon grated Parmesan cheese

Heat oil in 10-inch nonstick skillet over medium-high heat. Add chicken and garlic. Cook 15 to 20 minutes, turning once, until juice is no longer pink when centers of thickest pieces are cut. Remove chicken mixture from skillet; keep warm.

Heat remaining ingredients except vermicelli and cheese to boiling in same skillet. Cook and stir 3 to 4 minutes or until vegetables are crisp-tender. Stir in vermicelli; cook until hot. Serve chicken over vermicelli mixture. Sprinkle with cheese.

1 Serving: Calories 365 (Calories from Fat 90); Fat 10g (Saturated 3g); Cholesterol 50mg; Sodium 350mg; Carbohydrate 45g (Dietary Fiber 3g); Protein 26g.

Italian Chicken Skillet

MEXICAN CHICKEN MANICOTTI

4 SERVINGS

8 uncooked manicotti shells

1 1/2 cups cut-up cooked chicken or turkey

1 cup shredded carrots (1 1/2 medium)

1 cup ricotta cheese

2 tablespoons sliced green onions

2 tablespoons chopped fresh cilantro or parsley

1 clove garlic, finely chopped

1 cup salsa

1/4 cup shredded Monterey Jack cheese with jalapeño peppers (1 ounce)

Heat oven to 325°. Cook and drain manicotti shells as directed on package. Mix chicken, carrots, ricotta cheese, onions, cilantro and garlic. Fill manicotti shells with chicken mixture.

Place manicotti in ungreased rectangular pan, 13 × 9 × 2 inches. Pour salsa over manicotti. Sprinkle with Monterey Jack cheese. Cover and bake about 35 minutes or until hot in center.

1 Serving: Calories 355 (Calories from Fat 110); Fat 12g (Saturated 6g); Cholesterol 70mg; Sodium 580mg; Carbohydrate 36g (Dietary Fiber 4g); Protein 30g.

ORIENTAL CHICKEN SKILLET

4 SERVINGS

1 tablespoon vegetable oil

2 boneless, skinless chicken breast halves, cut into 1/4-inch strips

1 medium red bell pepper, chopped (1 cup)

1/2 cup sliced green onions

2 packages (3 ounces each) chicken-flavored ramen noodles

1 1/2 cups water

1 tablespoon soy sauce

3 cups thinly sliced napa (Chinese) cabbage (12 ounces)

2 tablespoons sunflower nuts or chopped lightly salted peanuts

Heat oil in 12-inch skillet over medium-high heat. Cook chicken, bell pepper and onions in oil 3 to 4 minutes, stirring occasionally, until chicken is light brown.

Crumble noodles. Stir noodles, seasonings from flavor packets, water and soy sauce into chicken mixture. Heat to boiling. Cook 3 to 4 minutes, stirring occasionally, until noodles are completely softened and tender.

Stir in cabbage. Cook 1 to 2 minutes, stirring occasionally, until cabbage is softened. Sprinkle with nuts.

1 Serving: Calories 325 (Calories from Fat 125); Fat 14g (Saturated 4g); Cholesterol 35mg; Sodium 1340mg; Carbohydrate 33g (Dietary Fiber 3g); Protein 20g.

Oriental Chicken Skillet

FETTUCCINE WITH CHICKEN AND SUN-DRIED TOMATO SAUCE

4 SERVINGS

1/4 cup coarsely chopped sun-dried tomatoes (not oil-packed)

1/2 cup chicken broth

1/2 cup sliced mushrooms (1 1/2 ounces)

2 tablespoons chopped green onions

2 cloves garlic, finely chopped

2 tablespoons dry red wine (or nonalcoholic) or chicken broth

1 tablespoon olive or vegetable oil

4 boneless, skinless chicken breast halves (about 1 pound)

4 ounces uncooked fettuccine

1/2 cup milk

2 teaspoons cornstarch

2 teaspoons chopped fresh or 1/2 teaspoon dried basil leaves

Mix tomatoes and broth; let stand 30 minutes.

Cook mushrooms, onions and garlic in wine in 10-inch skillet over medium heat about 3 minutes, stirring occasionally, until mushrooms are tender. Remove mushroom mixture from skillet.

Heat oil in same skillet over medium-high heat. Cook chicken in oil until brown on both sides. Add tomato mixture. Heat to boiling; reduce heat to low. Cover and simmer about 10 minutes, stirring occasionally, until juice of chicken is no longer pink when centers of thickest pieces are cut. Remove chicken from skillet; keep warm. Cook and drain fettuccine as directed on package.

Mix milk, cornstarch and basil; stir into tomato mixture in skillet. Heat to boiling, stirring constantly. Boil and stir 1 minute. Stir in mushroom mixture; cook until hot. Serve over chicken and fettuccine.

1 Serving: Calories 295 (Calories from Fat 80); Fat 9g (Saturated 2g); Cholesterol 95mg; Sodium 250mg; Carbohydrate 24g (Dietary Fiber 2g); Protein 32g.

TOMATO DIJON TURKEY WITH FETTUCCINE

6 SERVINGS

8 ounces uncooked fettuccine

1 tablespoon olive or vegetable oil

2 tablespoons margarine, butter or spread

1 pound turkey breast slices (about 1/4 inch thick)

3/4 teaspoon salt

1/4 teaspoon pepper

1 egg white, slightly beaten

2/3 cup dry bread crumbs

Tomato Dijon Salsa (right)

Cook and drain fettuccine as directed on package. Toss fettuccine and oil. Melt margarine in 12-inch skillet over medium heat. Sprinkle turkey with salt and pepper. Dip turkey into egg white, then coat with bread crumbs.

Cook turkey in margarine 3 to 4 minutes, turning once, until golden brown and no longer pink in center. Place fettuccine on serving platter. Arrange turkey on fettuccine. Top with Tomato Dijon Salsa.

TOMATO DIJON SALSA

**3 medium tomatoes, chopped
(about 2 1/4 cups)**

1 tablespoon chopped fresh chives

2 tablespoons olive or vegetable oil

1 tablespoon Dijon mustard

1 tablespoon red wine vinegar

1/4 teaspoon sugar

1 clove garlic, finely chopped

Mix all ingredients in glass or plastic bowl.

1 Serving: Calories 370 (Calories from Fat 135); Fat 15g
(Saturated 3g); Cholesterol 80mg; Sodium 510mg;
Carbohydrate 37g (Dietary Fiber 3g); Protein 25g.

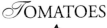

Tomatoes were introduced to Europe after they
were discovered in America, but were thought
to be poisonous, so were used only as ornamental plants. Neapolitans were the first to use
tomatoes as a food source, during a famine in
the seventeenth century. It is in this region
around Naples where wonderful pear-shaped
tomatoes are grown and canned. They make
excellent sauces, having more pulp, more
sweetness and lower acidity than other varieties
of tomatoes. This tomato is known by several
names: plum, pear-shaped or roma.

GARLIC CHICKEN AND MUSHROOMS

4 SERVINGS

*Without chicken, this becomes a delicious side dish,
especially nice with grilled meat.*

**2 1/4 cups uncooked mafalde (mini-lasagna
noodle) pasta (4 1/4 ounces)**

2 tablespoons olive or vegetable oil

**1 pound boneless, skinless chicken breast
halves, cut into 1/2-inch slices**

8 cloves garlic, finely chopped

8 ounces whole mushrooms, cut into fourths

1/2 cup sliced green onions (5 medium)

**1 can (14 1/2 ounces) diced tomatoes,
undrained**

1/2 cup chicken broth

1/2 teaspoon crushed red pepper

1/2 teaspoon cornstarch

1/2 teaspoon salt

1/2 cup chopped fresh cilantro or parsley

Cook and drain pasta as directed on package. Heat
1 tablespoon of the oil in 12-inch skillet over
medium-high heat. Cook chicken in oil 3 to 4
minutes, stirring occasionally, until light brown.
Remove chicken from skillet; keep warm.

Heat remaining 1 tablespoon oil in skillet over
medium-high heat. Cook garlic in oil, stirring
occasionally, until golden. Stir in mushrooms and
onions. Cook 2 minutes, stirring occasionally.

Stir in tomatoes, broth, red pepper, cornstarch and
salt. Heat to boiling; reduce heat to medium. Cook
4 to 5 minutes, stirring occasionally, until thickened. Stir in pasta, chicken and cilantro.

1 Serving: Calories 395 (Calories from Fat 100); Fat 11g
(Saturated 2g); Cholesterol 60mg; Sodium 600mg;
Carbohydrate 44g (Dietary Fiber 3g); Protein 33g.

CINCINNATI CHILI

6 SERVINGS

10 ounces uncooked spaghetti

1 tablespoon oil

1 pound lean ground turkey

1 medium onion, chopped (1/2 cup)

1 clove garlic, finely chopped

1 jar (26 to 28 ounces) chunky-style vegetable spaghetti sauce

1 can (15 to 16 ounces) kidney beans, rinsed and drained

2 tablespoons chili powder

1/2 cup shredded Cheddar cheese (2 ounces)

1/3 cup sliced green onions (4 medium)

Cook and drain spaghetti as directed on package. Heat oil in 10-inch skillet over medium heat. Cook turkey, onion and garlic in oil 5 to 6 minutes, stirring occasionally, until turkey is no longer pink.

Stir in spaghetti sauce, beans and chili powder; reduce heat to low. Cook 10 minutes, stirring occasionally. Serve sauce over spaghetti. Sprinkle with cheese and onions.

1 Serving: Calories 495 (Calories from Fat 155); Fat 17g (Saturated 5g); Cholesterol 60mg; Sodium 1180mg; Carbohydrate 63g (Dietary Fiber 8g); Protein 30g.

ITALIAN SAUSAGE SOUP

6 SERVINGS

This is a good, hearty soup to serve in winter. Serve it with a salad, crusty breadsticks and fresh apples for dessert.

1 pound turkey Italian sausage links, cut into 1-inch pieces

2 cups broccoli flowerets

1 cup uncooked mostaccioli pasta (3 ounces)

2 1/2 cups water

1/2 teaspoon dried basil leaves

1/4 teaspoon fennel seed, crushed

1/4 teaspoon pepper

1 can (28 ounces) whole Italian-style tomatoes, undrained

1 can (10 1/2 ounces) condensed beef broth

1 medium onion, chopped (1/2 cup)

1 clove garlic, finely chopped

Cook sausage in Dutch oven over medium-high heat, stirring occasionally, until brown; drain. Stir in remaining ingredients, breaking up tomatoes. Heat to boiling; reduce heat to medium-low. Cover and cook about 15 minutes, stirring occasionally, until mostaccioli is tender.

1 Serving: Calories 270 (Calories from Fat 80); Fat 9g (Saturated 3g); Cholesterol 55mg; Sodium 1220mg; Carbohydrate 27g (Dietary Fiber 3g); Protein 23g.

STRING PIE

6 SERVINGS

You'll like this fun and easy way to serve spaghetti.

4 ounces uncooked spaghetti

1 tablespoon margarine, butter or spread

1/2 pound ground turkey

1 small green bell pepper, chopped (1/2 cup)

1 small onion, chopped (1/4 cup)

1 jar (14 ounces) spaghetti sauce

1 teaspoon chili powder

1/2 teaspoon salt

1/4 teaspoon pepper

2 eggs

1 cup small curd creamed cottage cheese

1/2 cup shredded mozzarella cheese
(2 ounces)

Heat oven to 375°. Grease pie plate, 10 × 1 1/2 inches. Cook and drain spaghetti as directed on package. Place spaghetti in pie plate, pressing down gently.

Melt margarine in 10-inch skillet over medium-high heat. Cook turkey, bell pepper and onion in margarine, stirring occasionally, until turkey is no longer pink. Stir in spaghetti sauce, chili powder, salt and pepper; reduce heat to medium. Cook 5 to 6 minutes, stirring occasionally, until sauce is thickened.

Mix eggs and cottage cheese; spread evenly over spaghetti. Spoon turkey mixture over cottage cheese mixture. Sprinkle with mozzarella cheese. Bake 35 to 45 minutes or until center is set. Let stand 5 minutes before cutting.

1 Serving: Calories 300 (Calories from Fat 125); Fat 14g (Saturated 5g); Cholesterol 105mg; Sodium 890mg; Carbohydrate 25g (Dietary Fiber 2g); Protein 20g.

MEXICAN ORZO SKILLET

4 SERVINGS

1 pound ground turkey

1 cup salsa

1/2 cup uncooked rosamarina (orzo) pasta

1 cup water

1 tablespoon chopped fresh cilantro or
1 teaspoon ground coriander

1/4 teaspoon red pepper sauce

1 can (15 to 16 ounces) pinto beans, rinsed
and drained

Guacamole

Cook turkey in 10-inch skillet over medium heat, stirring occasionally, until no longer pink; drain. Stir in remaining ingredients except guacamole. Heat to boiling; reduce heat to low. Cover and simmer about 15 minutes, stirring frequently, until pasta is tender. Serve with guacamole.

1 Serving: Calories 405 (Calories from Fat 135); Fat 15g (Saturated 4g); Cholesterol 75mg; Sodium 770mg; Carbohydrate 42g (Dietary Fiber 9g); Protein 34g.

LINGUINE WITH CLAM SAUCE

4 SERVINGS

1 pint shucked fresh small clams, drained and liquid reserved*

1/4 cup olive or vegetable oil

3 cloves garlic, finely chopped

1 can (28 ounces) whole Italian-style tomatoes, drained and chopped

1 small red jalapeño chile, seeded and finely chopped

1 tablespoon chopped fresh parsley

1/2 teaspoon salt

1 package (16 ounces) linguine

Chopped fresh parsley

Chop clams. Heat oil in 10-inch skillet over medium-high heat. Cook garlic in oil, stirring frequently, until soft. Stir in tomatoes and chile. Cook 3 minutes. Stir in clam liquid. Heat to boiling; reduce heat to low. Simmer uncovered 10 minutes.

Stir in clams, 1 tablespoon parsley and salt. Cover and simmer about 30 minutes, stirring occasionally, until clams are tender.

Cook and drain linguine as directed on package. Mix linguine and sauce. Sprinkle with parsley.

2 cans (6 1/2 ounces each) minced clams, drained and liquid reserved, can be substituted for the fresh clams.

1 Serving: Calories 655 (Calories from Fat 155); Fat 17g (Saturated 2g); Cholesterol 25mg; Sodium 640mg; Carbohydrate 103g (Dietary Fiber 5g); Protein 27g.

PEANUTTY SHRIMP STIR-FRY

4 SERVINGS

1 cup coarsely broken uncooked vermicelli (about 2-inch pieces)

2 tablespoons soy sauce

2 teaspoons grated gingerroot

1/4 teaspoon red pepper sauce

1 clove garlic, finely chopped

1/2 pound fresh or frozen uncooked shrimp, peeled and deveined

3 tablespoons vegetable oil

4 green onions, cut into 1-inch pieces

1 package (6 ounces) frozen Chinese pea pods, thawed and drained

2 tablespoons creamy peanut butter

1/4 cup chopped peanuts

Cook and drain vermicelli as directed on package. Mix soy sauce, gingerroot, pepper sauce and garlic in large plastic resealable bag. Add shrimp; seal bag. Let stand 15 minutes.

Heat 2 tablespoons of the oil in 10-inch skillet over medium-high heat. Add vermicelli, onions and pea pods; stir-fry until onions are crisp-tender. Remove vermicelli mixture from skillet.

Heat remaining 1 tablespoon oil in same skillet over medium heat. Add shrimp; stir-fry until pink. Stir in vermicelli mixture. Mix in peanut butter until mixture is coated; cook until hot. Sprinkle with peanuts.

1 Serving: Calories 340 (Calories from Fat 170); Fat 19g (Saturated 3g); Cholesterol 80mg; Sodium 650mg; Carbohydrate 27g (Dietary Fiber 3g); Protein 18g.

VERMICELLI FRITTATA WITH CLAMS

6 SERVINGS

6 ounces uncooked vermicelli

2 cans (6 1/2 ounces each) minced clams, drained

1 tablespoon vegetable oil

1 small red bell pepper, chopped (1/2 cup)

2/3 cup sliced green onions (6 medium)

1 clove garlic, finely chopped

4 eggs

2 tablespoons milk

2 tablespoons grated Romano cheese

1/4 teaspoon salt

1/4 teaspoon pepper

Heat oven to 375°. Grease 10-inch pie plate. Cook and drain vermicelli as directed on package. Mix vermicelli and clams. Place in pie plate; press down slightly.

Heat oil in 8-inch skillet over medium heat. Cook bell pepper, onions and garlic in oil, stirring occasionally, until vegetables are crisp-tender. Spread evenly over vermicelli mixture.

Beat eggs, milk, cheese, salt and pepper. Pour over vegetables. Bake 20 to 25 minutes or until center is set. Let stand 5 minutes before cutting.

1 Serving: Calories 230 (Calories from Fat 65); Fat 7g (Saturated 2g); Cholesterol 160mg; Sodium 200mg; Carbohydrate 27g (Dietary Fiber 1g); Protein 16g.

CREAMY ITALIAN SHRIMP

4 SERVINGS

6 ounces uncooked linguine or fettuccine, broken into 3-inch pieces

2 tablespoons olive or vegetable oil

1 pound fresh or frozen uncooked medium shrimp, peeled and deveined

1 to 2 cloves garlic, finely chopped

2 small zucchini, cut lengthwise in half and thinly sliced (2 cups)

1 cup half-and-half

3/4 cup grated Parmesan cheese

1/4 cup pesto

1 tablespoon chopped fresh or 1 teaspoon dried rosemary leaves

2 teaspoons lemon juice

1/4 teaspoon pepper

2 medium tomatoes, seeded and cut into bite-size pieces

Cook and drain linguine as directed on package. Heat wok or 12-inch skillet over high heat until hot. Add 1 tablespoon of the oil to wok; rotate wok to coat side. Add shrimp and garlic; stir-fry about 3 minutes or until shrimp are pink; remove from wok.

Add remaining 1 tablespoon oil to wok; rotate wok to coat side. Add zucchini; stir-fry about 3 minutes or until crisp-tender. Stir in half-and-half, cheese, pesto, rosemary, lemon juice and pepper. Cook, stirring occasionally, until slightly thickened. Stir in shrimp mixture, linguine and tomatoes. Cook about 1 minute or until hot.

1 Serving: Calories 535 (Calories from Fat 260); Fat 29g (Saturated 10g); Cholesterol 145mg; Sodium 490mg; Carbohydrate 43g (Dietary Fiber 3g); Protein 28g.

Vermicelli Frittata with Clams

SHRIMP AND VEGETABLE SKEWERS

4 SERVINGS

In the summer, try these shrimp and vegetable skewers on an outdoor grill.

1 cup uncooked rosamarina (orzo) pasta
(6 ounces)

3 tablespoons sliced almonds, toasted

2 tablespoons grated Parmesan cheese

1 tablespoon chopped fresh or 1 teaspoon
dried basil leaves

2 teaspoons lemon juice

2 teaspoons margarine, butter or spread

16 fresh or frozen uncooked large shrimp,
peeled and deveined

1 small green bell pepper, cut into 1-inch
pieces

16 small whole mushrooms

1 small onion, cut into 1-inch pieces

2 tablespoons olive or vegetable oil

1 teaspoon dried basil leaves

1/4 teaspoon salt

4 lemon wedges

Paprika

Cook and drain pasta directed on package. Stir in almonds, cheese, 1 tablespoon basil, the lemon juice and margarine. Cover and keep warm.

Thread shrimp, bell pepper, mushrooms and onion alternately on each of four 10- to 12-inch metal skewers. Place on rack in broiler pan. Brush with oil. Sprinkle with basil and salt.

Set oven control to broil. Broil kabobs with tops 3 inches from heat 4 to 5 minutes, turning once, until shrimp are pink and vegetables are tender. Place orzo on serving platter. Top with kabobs. Garnish with lemon wedges. Sprinkle with paprika.

1 Serving: Calories 330 (Calories from Fat 125); Fat 14g (Saturated 2g); Cholesterol 55mg; Sodium 320mg; Carbohydrate 39g (Dietary Fiber 3g); Protein 15g.

SCAMPI WITH FETTUCCINE

4 SERVINGS

1 1/2 pounds fresh or frozen uncooked medium shrimp, peeled and deveined

2 tablespoons olive or vegetable oil

2 tablespoons thinly sliced green onions

1 tablespoon chopped fresh or 1/2 teaspoon dried basil leaves

1 tablespoon chopped fresh parsley

2 tablespoons lemon juice

1/4 teaspoon salt

2 cloves garlic, finely chopped

4 cups hot cooked fettuccine

Heat oil in 10-inch skillet over medium heat. Stir in shrimp and remaining ingredients except fettuccine. Cook 2 to 3 minutes, stirring frequently, until shrimp are pink; remove from heat. Toss fettuccine with shrimp mixture in skillet.

1 Serving: Calories 340 (Calories from Fat 90); Fat 10g (Saturated 2g); Cholesterol 215mg; Sodium 330mg; Carbohydrate 41g (Dietary Fiber 3g); Protein 25g.

SCALLOP STIR-FRY

4 SERVINGS

1 package (3 ounces) Oriental flavor ramen noodles

1 tablespoon olive or vegetable oil

12 ounces asparagus, cut into 1-inch pieces (2 1/2 cups)

1 large red bell pepper, cut into thin strips

1 small onion, chopped (1/4 cup)

2 cloves garlic, finely chopped

3/4 pound sea scallops, cut into 1-inch pieces

1 tablespoon soy sauce

2 tablespoons lemon juice

1 teaspoon sesame oil

1/4 teaspoon red pepper sauce

Reserve seasoning packet from noodles. Cook and drain noodles as directed on package. Heat olive oil in 12-inch skillet over high heat until hot. Add asparagus, bell pepper, onion and garlic; stir-fry 2 to 3 minutes or until vegetables are crisp-tender. Add scallops; stir-fry until white.

Mix contents of reserved seasoning packet, soy sauce, lemon juice, sesame oil and pepper sauce; stir into scallop mixture. Stir in noodles; cook until hot.

1 Serving: Calories 185 (Calories from Fat 65); Fat 7g (Saturated 1g); Cholesterol 25mg; Sodium 580mg; Carbohydrate 12g (Dietary Fiber 2g); Protein 21g.

Scallop Stir-fry

SCALLOPS TETRAZZINI

4 SERVINGS

6 ounces uncooked spaghetti, broken into 3-inch pieces

1 pound bay or sea scallops

1 1/2 cups water

1 tablespoon lemon juice

3 tablespoons margarine, butter or spread

2 cups sliced mushrooms (6 ounces)

1/2 cup sliced green onions (5 medium)

3 tablespoons all-purpose flour

3/4 teaspoon ground mustard (dry)

1/4 teaspoon salt

1/4 teaspoon pepper

1/4 teaspoon paprika

2 cups milk

1/4 cup grated Parmesan or Romano cheese

2 tablespoons dry sherry or chicken broth

1/4 cup grated Parmesan or Romano cheese

Heat oven to 350°. Cook and drain spaghetti as directed on package. If using sea scallops, cut into fourths. Mix scallops, water and lemon juice in 1 1/2-quart saucepan. Heat to boiling; reduce heat to low. Simmer uncovered 1 to 3 minutes or until scallops are white. Remove scallops from saucepan; reserve 1/2 cup liquid.

Melt margarine in same saucepan over medium heat. Cook mushrooms and onions in margarine, stirring occasionally, until onions are crisp-tender. Stir in flour, mustard, salt, pepper and paprika. Cook over medium heat, stirring constantly, until bubbly; remove from heat. Stir in milk and reserved liquid. Heat to boiling, stirring constantly. Boil and stir 1 minute. Stir in 1/4 cup cheese and the sherry.

Mix spaghetti, scallops and sauce in ungreased rectangular pan, 11×7×1 1/2 inches. Sprinkle with 1/4 cup cheese. Bake uncovered 25 to 30 minutes or until hot.

1 Serving: Calories 515 (Calories from Fat 155); Fat 17g (Saturated 5g); Cholesterol 55mg; Sodium 790mg; Carbohydrate 52g (Dietary Fiber 2g); Protein 41g.

SOUTHWEST SAUTÉED SCALLOPS

6 SERVINGS

2 cups water

1 dried Anaheim chile or 1 tablespoon canned chopped green chilies

2 tablespoons margarine, butter or spread

1/4 cup sliced green onions (3 medium)

2 tablespoons lime juice

2 pounds sea scallops

2 cups cubed fresh pineapple

1 cup Chinese pea pod halves (3 ounces)

3 cups hot cooked fettuccine

Heat water to boiling in 1-quart saucepan. Add chile. Boil 5 minutes; drain. Remove stem and seeds; finely chop chile.

Melt margarine in 10-inch skillet over medium heat. Cook onions, lime juice and chile in margarine, stirring occasionally, until onion is crisp-tender. Carefully stir in scallops. Cook over medium heat about 12 minutes, stirring occasionally, until scallops are white.

Stir in pineapple and pea pods; cook until hot. Remove scallop mixture with slotted spoon; keep warm.

Heat liquid in skillet to boiling. Boil until slightly thickened and reduced to about half. Spoon scallop mixture onto fettuccine. Pour liquid over scallop mixture.

1 Serving: Calories 345 (Calories from Fat 65); Fat 7g (Saturated 1g); Cholesterol 75mg; Sodium 450mg; Carbohydrate 34g (Dietary Fiber 2g); Protein 39g.

Mix broth, plum sauce and cornstarch. Stir into vegetables. Cook 1 to 2 minutes, stirring constantly, until sauce is thickened. Serve noodles over sauce. Sprinkle with chives.

1 Serving: Calories 200 (Calories from Fat 90); Fat 10g (Saturated 2g); Cholesterol 10mg; Sodium 370mg; Carbohydrate 24g (Dietary Fiber 2g); Protein 6g.

CRISPY CHINESE CRAB

6 SERVINGS

1/4 cup vegetable oil

1/2 package (5.3-ounce size) cellophane noodles (bean threads), crumbled

2 cups sliced mushrooms (6 ounces)

2 medium carrots, shredded (about 1 1/4 cups)

1 medium stalk celery, thinly sliced (1/2 cup)

1 small onion, chopped (1/4 cup)

6 ounces imitation crabmeat sticks, sliced

1/3 cup chicken broth

2 tablespoons Chinese plum sauce or plum preserves

1 teaspoon cornstarch

1 tablespoon chopped fresh chives

Heat 2 tablespoons of the oil in 12-inch skillet over medium-high heat. Cook half of the noodles in oil 2 to 3 minutes, until puffed and crisp; drain and keep warm. Repeat with remaining oil and noodles. Wipe skillet.

Cook mushrooms, carrots, celery and onion in skillet, stirring occasionally, until carrots and celery are crisp-tender. Stir in crab.

CAPELLINI WITH LOBSTER

4 SERVINGS

Béchamel Sauce (page 143)

6 ounces uncooked capellini (angel hair) pasta

1/2 cup shredded Monterey Jack cheese (2 ounces)

2 tablespoons grated Parmesan cheese

2 tablespoons dry white wine (or nonalcoholic) or chicken broth

1/2 cup sliced green onions (5 medium)

1/2 pound cooked lobster or imitation lobster, sliced

1 small red bell pepper, chopped (1/2 cup)

Prepare Béchamel Sauce. Cook and drain pasta as directed on package. Stir cheeses, wine and onions into Béchamel Sauce. Toss sauce, lobster and pasta. Sprinkle with bell pepper.

1 Serving: Calories 325 (Calories from Fat 80); Fat 9g (Saturated 4g); Cholesterol 55mg; Sodium 560mg; Carbohydrate 40g (Dietary Fiber 4g); Protein 25g.

GRECIAN FISH SUPREME

4 SERVINGS

2 cups uncooked ziti pasta (7 ounces)

1 tablespoon olive or vegetable oil

1/2 cup sliced green onions (5 medium)

2 cloves garlic, finely chopped

1 can (14 1/2 ounces) diced tomatoes,
     undrained

2 tablespoons dry red wine
     (or nonalcoholic)

1 medium green bell pepper, chopped
     (1 cup)

1/4 cup chopped fresh parsley

2 tablespoons chopped fresh or 2 teaspoons
     dried oregano leaves

1/2 teaspoon sugar

1/4 teaspoon salt

1/4 teaspoon pepper

4 small halibut, tuna or swordfish
     steaks, about 3/4 inch thick
     (about 1 1/2 pounds)

1/2 cup crumbled feta cheese (2 ounces)

1 tablespoon chopped fresh parsley

Cook and drain pasta as directed on package. Heat oil in 10-inch skillet over medium heat. Cook onions and garlic in oil, stirring occasionally, until onions are tender. Stir in tomatoes, wine, bell pepper, 1/4 cup parsley, the oregano, sugar, salt and pepper; reduce heat to low. Cover and simmer 15 minutes.

Add fish to skillet. Cover and simmer 8 to 10 minutes, turning once, until fish flakes easily with fork. Sprinkle cheese over fish. Cover and simmer 1 to 2 minutes or until cheese is melted. Serve fish and sauce over pasta. Sprinkle with 1 tablespoon parsley.

1 Serving: Calories 470 (Calories from Fat 100); Fat 11g (Saturated 4g); Cholesterol 105mg; Sodium 660mg; Carbohydrate 53g (Dietary Fiber 4g); Protein 44g.

FUSILLI WITH SMOKED SALMON

4 SERVINGS

The smoky flavor of this colorful dish is sure to be a hit!

1 cup Béchamel Sauce (page 143)

2 cups uncooked fusilli pasta (6 ounces)

2 teaspoons margarine, butter or spread

2 medium carrots, shredded
     (about 1 1/4 cups)

1 medium zucchini, cut into julienne strips

1 medium yellow bell pepper, cut into thin
     strips

1/2 cup shredded Gruyère or Swiss cheese
     (2 ounces)

1 tablespoon chopped fresh or 1/2 teaspoon
     dried dill weed

1 cup flaked smoked salmon

Prepare Béchamel Sauce. Cook and drain pasta as directed on package. Melt margarine in 10-inch skillet over medium-high heat. Cook carrots, zucchini and bell pepper in margarine, stirring occasionally, until vegetables are crisp-tender.

Stir cheese and dill weed into Béchamel Sauce until cheese is melted. Stir in salmon. Toss sauce, vegetables and pasta.

1 Serving: Calories 365 (Calories from Fat 110); Fat 12g (Saturated 4g); Cholesterol 40mg; Sodium 290mg; Carbohydrate 46g (Dietary Fiber 3g); Protein 21g.

Fusilli with Smoked Salmon

TUNA CUPS WITH PIMIENTO SAUCE

4 SERVINGS

Pimiento Sauce (below)

1/2 cup acini de pepe pasta (4 ounces)

1 tablespoon margarine, butter or spread

1 small onion, finely chopped (1/4 cup)

1/4 cup finely chopped celery

1 can (6 1/8 ounces) tuna, drained

3 tablespoons diced pimientos

2 tablespoons chopped fresh parsley

1/4 cup mayonnaise or salad dressing

1 egg, slightly beaten

3/4 teaspoon lemon pepper

1 tablespoon chopped fresh parsley

Prepare Pimiento Sauce. Heat oven to 350°. Grease four 6-ounce custard cups. Cook and drain pasta as directed on package.

Melt margarine in 10-inch skillet over medium heat. Cook onion and celery in margarine, stirring occasionally, until tender. Stir in pasta, tuna, pimientos, 2 tablespoons parsley, the mayonnaise, egg and lemon pepper.

Spoon tuna mixture into custard cups; place on cookie sheet. Bake 25 to 30 minutes or until light brown. If desired, tuna cups can be unmolded to serve. Spoon sauce over tuna cups; sprinkle with 1 tablespoon parsley.

PIMIENTO SAUCE

1/3 cup mayonnaise or salad dressing

1 tablespoon diced pimientos

1/2 teaspoon lemon juice

Mix all ingredients in glass or plastic bowl. Cover and refrigerate 30 minutes to blend flavors.

1 Serving: Calories 265 (Calories from Fat 100); Fat 11g (Saturated 2g); Cholesterol 65mg; Sodium 280mg; Carbohydrate 25g (Dietary Fiber 1g); Protein 18g.

TUNA NOODLES ROMANOFF

6 SERVINGS

4 cups uncooked egg noodles (8 ounces)

2 cans (6 1/8 ounces each) tuna, drained

1 jar (2 ounces) diced pimientos, drained

1 cup sliced mushrooms (3 ounces)

1 1/2 cups sour cream

3/4 cup milk

1 tablespoon chopped fresh chives

1 teaspoon salt

1/4 teaspoon pepper

1/4 cup dry bread crumbs

1/4 cup grated Romano cheese

2 tablespoons margarine, butter or spread, melted

Heat oven to 350°. Cook and drain noodles as directed on package. Mix noodles, tuna, pimientos, mushrooms, sour cream, milk, chives, salt and pepper in ungreased 2-quart casserole or square baking dish, 8 × 8 × 2 inches.

Mix bread crumbs, cheese and margarine; sprinkle over tuna mixture. Bake uncovered 35 to 40 minutes or until hot and bubbly.

1 Serving: Calories 405 (Calories from Fat 205); Fat 23g (Saturated 10g); Cholesterol 80mg; Sodium 750mg; Carbohydrate 26g (Dietary Fiber 1g); Protein 25g.

CITRUS FISH AND SPINACH STIR-FRY

4 SERVINGS

4 ounces uncooked spaghetti, broken into 3-inch pieces

1 pound halibut, tuna, monkfish or swordfish steaks

1/2 cup orange juice

1/2 cup dry sherry or water

1 tablespoon cornstarch

1 tablespoon chopped fresh or 1 teaspoon dried basil leaves

1 1/2 teaspoons chopped fresh or 1/2 teaspoon dried marjoram leaves

1/2 teaspoon salt

1/8 teaspoon pepper

2 tablespoons vegetable oil

3 medium carrots, thinly sliced (1 1/2 cups)

1 large onion, sliced

4 cups bite-size pieces spinach

Cook and drain spaghetti as directed on package. Remove any skin and bones from fish. Cut fish into 1-inch pieces. Mix orange juice, sherry, cornstarch, basil, marjoram, salt and pepper.

Heat wok or 12-inch skillet over high heat until very hot. Add 1 tablespoon of the oil to wok; rotate wok to coat side. Add carrots and onion; stir-fry about 5 minutes or until crisp-tender. Remove carrot mixture from wok.

Add remaining 1 tablespoon oil to wok; rotate wok to coat side. Add fish; gently stir-fry about 4 minutes, trying to keep fish pieces intact, until fish flakes easily with fork. Carefully remove fish from wok.

Add orange juice mixture to wok. Cook and stir about 1 minute or until thickened. Stir in carrot mixture, fish, spaghetti and spinach. Cook about 1 minute or until mixture is hot and spinach just starts to wilt.

1 Serving: Calories 340 (Calories from Fat 80); Fat 9g (Saturated 1g); Cholesterol 60mg; Sodium 430mg; Carbohydrate 42g (Dietary Fiber 5g); Protein 28g.

5

MEATLESS

Manicotti (p. 145)
Olive Crostini (p. 175)

PASTA PRIMAVERA

4 SERVINGS

8 ounces uncooked fettuccine or linguine

1 tablespoon olive or vegetable oil

1 cup broccoli flowerets

1 cup cauliflowerets

2 medium carrots, thinly sliced (1 cup)

1 cup frozen green peas

1 small onion, chopped (1/4 cup)

1 container (10 ounces) Alfredo sauce

1 tablespoon grated Parmesan cheese

Cook and drain fettuccine as directed on package. Heat oil in 12-inch skillet over medium-high heat. Cook broccoli, cauliflowerets, carrots, peas and onion in oil 6 to 8 minutes, stirring frequently, until vegetables are crisp-tender.

Stir in Alfredo sauce; cook until hot. Stir in fettuccine; cook until hot. Sprinkle with cheese.

1 Serving: Calories 615 (Calories from Fat 370); Fat 41g (Saturated 21g); Cholesterol 155mg; Sodium 410mg; Carbohydrate 54g (Dietary Fiber 7g); Protein 15g.

MOSTACCIOLI WITH SUN-DRIED TOMATO PESTO

6 SERVINGS

3 cups uncooked mostaccioli pasta (9 ounces)

Sun-dried Tomato Pesto (below)

1/2 cup feta cheese, crumbled (4 ounces)

Cook and drain pasta as directed on package. Prepare Sun-dried Tomato Pesto. Toss pasta, pesto and cheese.

SUN-DRIED TOMATO PESTO

1/3 cup oil-packed sun-dried tomatoes, drained

1/4 cup firmly packed fresh mint leaves or 4 teaspoons dried mint leaves

2 tablespoons chopped walnuts

2 tablespoons tomato paste

1 tablespoon olive or vegetable oil

1 teaspoon lemon juice

1/2 teaspoon pepper

1 clove garlic

Place all ingredients in food processor or blender. Cover and process until mixture is almost smooth.

1 Serving: Calories 335 (Calories from Fat 80); Fat 9g (Saturated 3g); Cholesterol 10mg; Sodium 200mg; Carbohydrate 54g (Dietary Fiber 2g); Protein 11g.

Mostaccioli with Sun-dried Tomato Pesto

FETTUCCINE ALFREDO

4 SERVINGS

Fresh Pasta (page 18)*

2 tablespoons margarine, butter or spread

1 1/2 cups whipping (heavy) cream or half-and-half

1 tablespoon all-purpose flour

1/4 teaspoon salt

1/8 teaspoon pepper

2 tablespoons shredded Parmesan cheese

1/2 teaspoon freshly grated or 1/8 teaspoon ground nutmeg

4 quarts water

2 tablespoons shredded Parmesan cheese

Freshly grated nutmeg, if desired

Freshly ground pepper

Prepare dough for Fresh Pasta and roll as directed on page 22. Cut into fettuccine as directed. Remove one-third of the fettuccine and store for another use.

Melt margarine in 3-quart saucepan over medium-high heat. Mix whipping cream, flour, salt and pepper until smooth; pour into saucepan. Heat to boiling. Boil 1 minute, stirring frequently with wire whisk; remove from heat. Stir in 2 table-spoons cheese and 1/2 teaspoon nutmeg.

Heat water to boiling in 6- to 8-quart saucepan; add fettuccine. Boil uncovered 2 to 4 minutes, stir-ring occasionally, until firm but tender. Begin test-ing for doneness when fettuccine rises to surface of water. Drain fettuccine. Mix fettuccine and sauce. Sprinkle with 2 tablespoons cheese and the nut-meg. Serve with pepper.

*1 package (16 ounces) dry fettuccine can be sub-stituted for the Fresh Pasta. Cook and drain as directed on package.

1 Serving: Calories 715 (Calories from Fat 350); Fat 39g (Saturated 20g); Cholesterol 200mg; Sodium 340mg; Carbohydrate 78g (Dietary Fiber 5g); Protein 18g.

TRIPLE CHEESE RAVIOLI

4 SERVINGS

1 package (9 ounces) refrigerated cheese-filled ravioli or tortellini

2 large tomatoes, chopped (2 cups)

1/2 cup sliced mushrooms (1 1/2 ounces)

1 small onion, chopped (1/4 cup)

1/4 cup dry red wine (or nonalcoholic) or chicken broth

1 tablespoon chopped fresh or 1 teaspoon dried basil leaves

1/8 teaspoon salt

1/8 teaspoon pepper

1 clove garlic, finely chopped

1/2 cup ricotta cheese

2 tablespoons grated Parmesan cheese

Heat oven to 325°. Cook and drain ravioli as directed on package. Cook remaining ingredients except cheeses in 10-inch skillet over medium-high heat about 5 minutes, stirring frequently, until tomatoes are soft.

Place ravioli in ungreased square baking dish, 8 × 8 × 2 inches. Spread ricotta cheese over ravioli. Pour tomato mixture over top. Sprinkle with Parmesan cheese. Bake uncovered 20 to 25 min-utes or until hot.

1 Serving: Calories 150 (Calories from Fat 45); Fat 5g (Saturated 3g); Cholesterol 15mg; Sodium 510mg; Carbohydrate 19g (Dietary Fiber 2g); Protein 9g.

SAVORY FUSILLI

6 SERVINGS

1/4 cup olive or vegetable oil

1 tablespoon capers

3 cloves garlic, finely chopped

2 cans (28 ounces each) whole Italian-style tomatoes, drained and chopped

1 small red jalapeño chile, seeded and chopped

1/2 cup sliced imported Kalamata or ripe olives

1/2 cup sliced pimiento-stuffed olives

1 tablespoon chopped fresh or 1 teaspoon dried oregano leaves

1 tablespoon chopped fresh or 1 teaspoon dried basil leaves

1 package (16 ounces) long fusilli or rotini pasta

Freshly ground pepper

Heat oil in 10-inch skillet over medium-high heat. Cook capers and garlic in oil, stirring frequently, until garlic is soft. Stir in tomatoes and chile. Heat to boiling; reduce heat to low. Cover and simmer 20 minutes, stirring occasionally. Stir in olives, oregano and basil. Cover and simmer 10 minutes.

Cook and drain pasta as directed on package. Mix pasta and tomato mixture. Serve with pepper.

1 Serving: Calories 450 (Calories from Fat 125); Fat 14g (Saturated 2g); Cholesterol 0mg; Sodium 830mg; Carbohydrate 73g (Dietary Fiber 5g); Protein 13g.

BROCCOLI-MUSHROOM SPAGHETTI

5 SERVINGS

1 package (7 ounces) spaghetti

1 package (10 ounces) frozen chopped broccoli

1 jar (4 1/2 ounces) sliced mushrooms, drained

1/4 cup margarine, butter or spread

1/2 teaspoon salt

1/8 teaspoon pepper

1/2 cup grated Parmesan cheese

1 tablespoon lemon juice

Cook and drain spaghetti as directed on package. Cook and drain broccoli as directed on package.

Stir mushrooms, margarine, salt and pepper into broccoli. Cook over low heat about 5 minutes, stirring occasionally, until mushrooms are hot. Toss spaghetti, broccoli mixture, cheese and lemon juice. Serve with additional grated Parmesan cheese if desired.

1 Serving: Calories 285 (Calories from Fat 110); Fat 12g (Saturated 4g); Cholesterol 5mg; Sodium 580mg; Carbohydrate 36g (Dietary Fiber 3g); Protein 11g.

SPAGHETTI WITH CARAMELIZED ONIONS

6 SERVINGS

Cooking onions slowly to caramelize them adds a delectable sweetness, which is complemented by the earthy flavor of herbs.

8 ounces uncooked spaghetti

1 tablespoon olive or vegetable oil

1 tablespoon margarine, butter or spread

4 large onions, coarsely chopped (4 cups)

1/2 teaspoon dried thyme leaves

1/4 teaspoon dried rosemary leaves, crushed

1 cup frozen green peas, thawed

1 medium tomato, chopped (3/4 cup)

2 tablespoons balsamic vinegar

1/2 teaspoon salt

Cook and drain spaghetti as directed on package. Heat oil and margarine in 10-inch skillet over medium heat. Cook onions, thyme and rosemary in oil mixture 12 to 15 minutes, stirring occasionally, until onions are golden brown. Stir in peas, tomato, vinegar and salt. Toss with pasta.

1 Serving: Calories 230 (Calories from Fat 45); Fat 5g (Saturated 1g); Cholesterol 0mg; Sodium 220mg; Carbohydrate 43g (Dietary Fiber 4g); Protein 7g.

GARDEN VEGETABLE SPAGHETTI

6 SERVINGS

1 package (16 ounces) spaghetti

2 tablespoons olive or vegetable oil

2 medium carrots, sliced (2 cups)

1 medium onion, diced (1/2 cup)

1 medium stalk celery, thinly sliced (1/2 cup)

1 small eggplant (12 ounces), diced (3 1/2 cups)

1/2 clove garlic, finely chopped

3 medium tomatoes, cut into 1-inch pieces

1/2 cup frozen peas, thawed

2 tablespoons chopped fresh parsley

1 1/2 teaspoons chopped fresh or 1/2 teaspoon dried basil leaves

3/4 teaspoon chopped fresh or 1/4 teaspoon dried tarragon leaves

1/2 teaspoon salt

1/4 teaspoon pepper

2/3 cup grated Parmesan cheese

Cook and drain spaghetti as directed on package. Heat oil in 10-inch skillet over medium-high heat until hot. Cook carrots, onion, celery, eggplant and garlic in oil until vegetables are crisp-tender, stirring frequently. Stir in remaining ingredients except spaghetti and cheese. Cook until hot. Serve sauce over spaghetti. Sprinkle with cheese.

1 Serving: Calories 370 (Calories from Fat 45); Fat 5g (Saturated 2g); Cholesterol 5mg; Sodium 360mg; Carbohydrate 71g (Dietary Fiber 5g); Protein 15g.

Garden Vegetable Spaghetti

MUSHROOMS PAPRIKASH

6 SERVINGS

Use fresh dill if possible—it imparts a lively flavor and aroma to the dish.

4 cups uncooked egg noodles (8 ounces)

1 tablespoon margarine, butter or spread

1 pound mushrooms, thinly sliced (6 cups)

2 cloves garlic, finely chopped

4 teaspoons paprika

1/2 teaspoon salt

1/8 teaspoon pepper

1 cup sour cream

1/4 cup milk

2 tablespoons chopped fresh or 2 teaspoons dried dill weed

1/2 cup shredded Cheddar cheese (2 ounces)

Cook and drain noodles as directed on package. Melt margarine in 10-inch skillet over medium heat. Cook mushrooms, garlic, paprika, salt and pepper in margarine, stirring occasionally, until mushrooms are tender and most of liquid has evaporated.

Mix sour cream, milk and dill weed. Stir into mushroom mixture; cook until hot. Pour sauce over noodles. Toss with cheese until noodles are well coated.

1 Serving: Calories 285 (Calories from Fat 135); Fat 15g (Saturated 7g); Cholesterol 70mg; Sodium 290mg; Carbohydrate 31g (Dietary Fiber 3g); Protein 10g.

FARFALLE WITH MUSHROOM-CILANTRO SAUCE

4 SERVINGS

3 1/2 cups uncooked farfalle (bow tie) pasta (7 ounces)

3 tablespoons chopped fresh cilantro or parsley

2 teaspoons margarine, butter or spread

2 cups sliced mushrooms (4 ounces)

1/4 cup milk

1/4 cup dry white wine (or nonalcoholic) or chicken broth

2 tablespoons finely chopped oil-packed sun-dried tomatoes, drained

1/2 package (8-ounce size) cream cheese, softened

Cook and drain pasta as directed on package. Toss pasta and cilantro; keep warm.

Melt margarine in 10-inch skillet over medium heat. Cook mushrooms in margarine, stirring occasionally, until tender; reduce heat to low. Stir in remaining ingredients; cook until hot. Toss with pasta.

1 Serving: Calories 554 (Calories from Fat 125); Fat 14g (Saturated 7g); Cholesterol 30mg; Sodium 150mg; Carbohydrate 92g (Dietary Fiber 3g); Protein 18g.

Farfalle with Mushroom-Cilantro Sauce

BABA GHANOUSH WITH ROTINI

6 SERVINGS

A favorite Middle Eastern eggplant and tahini spread, Baba Ghanoush usually is served as an appetizer. Here it becomes a tasty combination with pasta.

1 medium eggplant (12 ounces)

3 1/2 cups uncooked rotini pasta
(9 1/2 ounces)

1/4 cup plain yogurt

3 tablespoons lemon juice

2 tablespoons grated Parmesan cheese

2 tablespoons chopped fresh parsley

2 tablespoons tahini (sesame paste)

2 tablespoons dry sherry or chicken broth

1 tablespoon olive or vegetable oil

2 cloves garlic, finely chopped

1/2 teaspoon salt

1/8 teaspoon ground red pepper (cayenne)

1 medium tomato, chopped (3/4 cup)

1 tablespoon chopped fresh parsley

Heat oven to 400°. Pierce eggplant with fork in several places and place in baking dish. Bake 50 to 60 minutes or until eggplant is tender; cool. Cook and drain pasta as directed on package.

Mix yogurt, lemon juice, cheese, 2 tablespoons parsley, the tahini, sherry, oil, garlic, salt and red pepper. When eggplant is cool enough to handle, remove skin and coarsely chop pulp. Mix eggplant and yogurt mixture. Toss with pasta. Garnish with tomato and 1 tablespoon parsley.

1 Serving: Calories 375 (Calories from Fat 65); Fat 7g (Saturated 1g); Cholesterol 2mg; Sodium 230mg; Carbohydrate 69g (Dietary Fiber 4g); Protein 13g.

FETTUCCINE WITH WILD MUSHROOMS

4 SERVINGS

1 cup hot water

1 package (about 1 ounce) dried porcini or cèpe mushrooms

2 tablespoons olive or vegetable oil

1 small onion, chopped (1/4 cup)

2 cloves garlic, finely chopped

1 cup whipping (heavy) cream

1/2 teaspoon salt

8 ounces uncooked fettuccine

Coarsely ground pepper

Pour water over mushrooms. Let stand 30 minutes; drain. Coarsely chop mushrooms.

Heat oil in 10-inch skillet over medium heat. Cook mushrooms, onion and garlic in oil, stirring occasionally, until onion is tender. Stir in whipping cream and salt. Heat to boiling; reduce heat to low. Simmer uncovered 3 to 5 minutes, stirring occasionally, until slightly thickened.

Cook and drain fettuccine as directed on package. Pour sauce over fettuccine; toss until fettuccine is well coated. Serve with pepper.

1 Serving: Calories 430 (Calories from Fat 245); Fat 27g (Saturated 13g); Cholesterol 115mg; Sodium 300mg; Carbohydrate 41g (Dietary Fiber 3g); Protein 9g.

VERMICELLI WITH LEMONY GREEN VEGETABLES

4 SERVINGS

1 package (7 ounces) vermicelli

2 tablespoons margarine, butter or spread

4 cups mixed bite-size pieces green vegetables (asparagus, broccoli, Chinese pea pods, green beans, zucchini)

1 tablespoon grated lemon peel

1/2 cup milk

1 package (3 ounces) cream cheese, softened

1/2 cup grated Parmesan cheese

1/4 teaspoon pepper

Cook and drain vermicelli as directed on package. Melt margarine in 10-inch skillet over medium-high heat. Cook vegetables in margarine, stirring frequently, until crisp-tender. Toss vegetables and lemon peel. Remove vegetables from skillet; keep warm.

Heat milk and cream cheese in same skillet over medium heat, stirring frequently, until smooth and creamy. Stir in Parmesan cheese and pepper. Toss with vermicelli. Serve vegetables over vermicelli.

1 Serving: Calories 405 (Calories from Fat 160); Fat 18g (Saturated 8g); Cholesterol 35mg; Sodium 350mg; Carbohydrate 49g (Dietary Fiber 4g); Protein 16g.

PASTA WITH THREE CHEESES

6 SERVINGS

2 tablespoons margarine, butter or spread

2 tablespoons all-purpose flour

1/2 teaspoon salt

1/8 teaspoon pepper

2 cups milk

1 cup shredded Fontina or mozzarella cheese (4 ounces)

1 cup shredded Gruyère or Swiss cheese (4 ounces)

1/2 cup grated Parmesan cheese

6 cups uncooked egg noodles (12 ounces)

3 tablespoons dry bread crumbs

1 tablespoon margarine, butter or spread, melted

Heat oven to 350°. Grease 2-quart casserole. Melt 2 tablespoons margarine in 2-quart saucepan over low heat. Stir in flour, salt and pepper. Cook over low heat, stirring constantly, until smooth and bubbly; remove from heat. Gradually stir in milk. Heat to boiling, stirring constantly. Boil and stir 1 minute. Stir in cheeses; remove from heat.

Cook and drain noodles as directed on package. Mix noodles and sauce in large bowl. Spoon into casserole. Mix bread crumbs and 1 tablespoon melted margarine; sprinkle over noodles.

Bake uncovered 20 to 30 minutes or until hot and bubbly.

1 Serving: Calories 435 (Calories from Fat 200); Fat 22g (Saturated 10g); Cholesterol 85mg; Sodium 610mg; Carbohydrate 40g (Dietary Fiber 2g); Protein 21g.

MACARONI, TOMATO AND SMOKED CHEESE

6 SERVINGS

2 cups Béchamel Sauce (page 143)

1 package (7 ounces) elbow macaroni (2 cups)

1 can (14 1/2 ounces) diced tomatoes, undrained

1 cup shredded smoked Gouda or Swiss cheese (4 ounces)

Heat oven to 350°. Grease 1 1/2-quart casserole. Prepare Béchamel Sauce as directed—except double ingredients to yield 2 cups sauce. Cook and drain macaroni as directed on package.

Heat tomatoes to boiling in 2-quart saucepan; reduce heat to medium. Cook uncovered 6 to 8 minutes, stirring occasionally, until liquid has evaporated. Stir cheese into Béchamel Sauce until melted. Stir in tomatoes.

Mix sauce and pasta. Pour into casserole. Bake uncovered about 30 minutes or until bubbly and light brown.

1 Serving: Calories 320 (Calories from Fat 90); Fat 10g (Saturated 4g); Cholesterol 20mg; Sodium 560mg; Carbohydrate 45g (Dietary Fiber 2g); Protein 14g.

RICE NOODLES WITH PEANUT SAUCE

4 SERVINGS

8 ounces uncooked rice stick noodles

1/2 cup creamy peanut butter

2 tablespoons soy sauce

1 teaspoon grated gingerroot

1/2 teaspoon crushed red pepper

1/2 cup chicken broth or water

4 ounces bean sprouts

1 small red bell pepper, cut into 1/4-inch strips

2 green onions, sliced

2 tablespoons chopped fresh cilantro, if desired

Heat 2 quarts water to boiling. Break noodles in half and pull apart slightly; drop into boiling water. Cook uncovered 1 minute; drain. Rinse with cold water; drain.

Mix peanut butter, soy sauce, gingerroot and red pepper with wire whisk in small bowl until smooth. Gradually whisk in broth. Place noodles in large bowl. Add peanut butter mixture, bean sprouts, bell pepper and onions; toss. Sprinkle with cilantro.

1 Serving: Calories 335 (Calories from Fat 145); Fat 16g (Saturated 3g); Cholesterol 0mg; Sodium 770mg; Carbohydrate 40g (Dietary Fiber 3g); Protein 11g.

Rice Noodles with Peanut Sauce

EASY AND DELICIOUS REDUCED-FAT SAUCES

Today's interest in healthful living is more than just a passing fad. People are looking for ways to incorporate their favorite foods into a healthier eating plan without sacrificing flavor. If you simply can't pass up pasta with creamy white sauces or robust tomato and meat sauces, we have good news for you! Making scrumptious, lower-fat sauces is probably easier than you imagine. Our intent wasn't to create "diet" sauces, but rather to cut back on some of the unnecessary fat and still have a great-tasting sauce. Three basic methods were used to reduce fat:

- We reduced the amount of high-fat ingredients such as oil, butter, cheese and nuts.

- We substituted lower-fat products for regular, full-fat products such as using evaporated or skim milk in place of whipping cream, nonstick cooking spray versus oil or butter and using extra lean meats or turkey products versus full-fat meats.

- We boosted flavors with herbs and spices or ingredients such as butter-flavored sprinkles. We chose four classic pasta sauce recipes and modified them to reduce the overall fat, yet retain all their wonderful flavors. The recipes we selected were Basil Pesto, Tomato Cream Sauce, Béchamel Sauce and Bolognese Sauce. One taste of these flavorful sauces will have you convinced—you won't miss all that extra fat!

BASIL PESTO

ABOUT **1** CUP PESTO

The original recipe used 1/2 cup Parmesan cheese, 1/2 cup pine nuts and 1/2 cup olive oil.

1 cup chopped fresh basil leaves

1/2 cup chopped fresh parsley

1/4 cup freshly grated shredded Parmesan cheese

1/4 cup pine nuts, toasted

1/4 cup olive or vegetable oil

1/4 cup chicken or vegetable broth

3/4 teaspoon salt

1/4 teaspoon pepper

3 cloves garlic

Place all ingredients in food processor or blender. Cover and process until smooth. Use sauce immediately, or cover and refrigerate up to 5 days or freeze up to 1 month.

1/4 Cup: Calories 100 (Calories from Fat 90); Fat 10g (Saturated 2g); Cholesterol 2mg; Sodium 280mg; Carbohydrate 2g (Dietary Fiber 1g); Protein 2g.

Tomato Cream Sauce

About 2 cups sauce

The original recipe used 1 tablespoon olive oil and 1/2 cup whipping cream.

1 medium onion, chopped (1/2 cup)

1 clove garlic, finely chopped

1 tablespoon chopped fresh parsley
   or 1 teaspoon dried parsley
   flakes

1 tablespoon chopped fresh or
   1 teaspoon dried basil leaves

1 can (28 ounces) whole Italian-style
   tomatoes, drained and chopped

1/2 cup evaporated milk

1/4 teaspoon salt

1/8 teaspoon pepper

Spray 12-inch nonstick skillet with nonstick cooking spray; heat over medium-high heat 30 seconds. Cook onion, garlic, parsley, basil and tomatoes in skillet 10 minutes, stirring occasionally.

Stir in remaining ingredients; reduce heat to low. Cook 15 to 20 minutes, stirring occasionally, until sauce is thickened. Use sauce immediately, or cover and refrigerate up to 24 hours.

1/2 Cup: Calories 80 (Calories from Fat 20); Fat 2g (Saturated 1g); Cholesterol 5mg; Sodium 490mg; Carbohydrate 15g (Dietary Fiber 3g); Protein 4g.

Béchamel Sauce

1 cup sauce

The original recipe used 2 tablespoons margarine and whole milk.

1 tablespoon margarine, butter or
   spread

1 cup skim milk

2 tablespoons all-purpose flour

1/4 teaspoon salt

1/8 teaspoon pepper

1 teaspoon butter-flavored sprinkles

Heat margarine in 1 1/2-quart saucepan over medium heat until melted and bubbly. Shake milk, flour, salt and pepper in tightly covered container. Gradually stir into margarine. Heat to boiling, stirring constantly. Boil and stir 1 minute. Stir in butter-flavored sprinkles.

1/4 Cup: Calories 60 (Calories from Fat 25); Fat 3g (Saturated 1g); Cholesterol 0mg; Sodium 200mg; Carbohydrate 6g (Dietary Fiber 0g); Protein 2g.

(Continued on next page)

BOLOGNESE SAUCE

ABOUT 6 CUPS SAUCE

The original recipe used 2 tablespoons each olive oil and margarine, 1/2 pound each regular Italian sausage and ground beef, and 1 teaspoon of salt.

1 teaspoon olive or vegetable oil

1 teaspoon margarine, butter or spread

2 medium carrots, finely chopped (1 cup)

1 medium onion, chopped (1/2 cup)

1/2 pound bulk turkey Italian sausage

1/2 pound extra lean ground beef

1/2 cup dry red wine or (or non-alcoholic) or beef broth

3 cans (28 ounces each) whole Italian-style tomatoes, drained and chopped

1 teaspoon dried oregano leaves

1/2 teaspoon pepper

Heat oil and margarine in 12-inch non-stick skillet over medium-high heat. Cook carrots and onion in oil mixture, stirring frequently, until crisp-tender. Stir in sausage and beef. Cook, stirring occasionally, until beef is brown and sausage is no longer pink; drain.

Stir in wine. Heat to boiling; reduce heat to low. Simmer uncovered until wine has evaporated. Stir in remaining ingredients. Heat to boiling; reduce heat to low. Cover and simmer 45 minutes, stirring occasionally. Use sauce immediately, or cover and refrigerate up to 48 hours or freeze up to 2 months.

1/2 Cup: Calories 150 (Calories from Fat 80); Fat 9g (Saturated 3g); Cholesterol 25mg; Sodium 515mg; Carbohydrate 11g (Dietary Fiber 2g); Protein 9g.

VEGETABLE MANICOTTI

4 SERVINGS

2 cups Béchamel Sauce (page 143)

8 uncooked manicotti shells

2 tablespoons grated Romano cheese

2 teaspoons chopped fresh or 1/2 teaspoon dried dill weed

1 tablespoon margarine, butter or spread

3 medium zucchini, shredded (4 cups)

1 large red bell pepper, chopped (1 1/2 cups)

1/2 cup sliced green onions (5 medium)

3/4 teaspoon salt

1/4 teaspoon pepper

3/4 cup ricotta cheese

Heat oven to 350°. Grease rectangular baking dish, 12 × 8 × 2 inches. Prepare Béchamel Sauce as directed—except double ingredients to yield 2 cups sauce. Cook and drain manicotti as directed on package. Rinse with cold water; drain. Stir Romano cheese and dill weed into sauce.

Melt margarine in 12-inch skillet over medium heat. Cook zucchini, bell pepper, onions, salt and pepper in margarine, stirring occasionally, until vegetables are crisp-tender. Stir in ricotta cheese. Heat 1 minute.

Fill manicotti with vegetable mixture. Place in baking dish. Pour sauce over manicotti. Cover and bake 30 to 40 minutes or until hot.

1 Serving: Calories 370 (Calories from Fat 125); Fat 14g (Saturated 5g); Cholesterol 20mg; Sodium 940mg; Carbohydrate 47g (Dietary Fiber 4g); Protein 18g.

MANICOTTI

5 SERVINGS

10 manicotti shells (from 8-ounce package)

1 can (15 ounces) tomato sauce

1 large tomato, chopped (1 cup)

1 tablespoon chopped fresh or 1 teaspoon dried basil leaves

2 cups small curd creamed cottage cheese

1/4 cup grated Parmesan cheese

1 teaspoon chopped fresh or 1/2 teaspoon dried thyme leaves

1 small onion, chopped (1/4 cup)

1 clove garlic, finely chopped

2 eggs

1 package (10 ounces) frozen chopped spinach, thawed and squeezed to drain

1 cup shredded mozzarella cheese (4 ounces)

Heat oven to 350°. Grease rectangular baking dish, 13 × 9 × 2 inches. Cook and drain manicotti as directed on package. Mix tomato sauce, tomato and basil. Spread 1 cup tomato sauce mixture evenly in baking dish.

Mix remaining ingredients except mozzarella cheese. Fill manicotti with spinach mixture. Place in baking dish. Pour remaining tomato sauce mixture over shells. Sprinkle with mozzarella cheese. Cover and bake 15 minutes; uncover and bake 15 to 20 minutes, or until hot and bubbly.

1 Serving: Calories 365 (Calories from Fat 110); Fat 12g (Saturated 6g); Cholesterol 115mg; Sodium 1110mg; Carbohydrate 40g (Dietary Fiber 4g); Protein 28g.

LASAGNA PRIMAVERA

8 SERVINGS

12 uncooked lasagna noodles

4 cups Béchamel Sauce (page 143) or prepared Alfredo sauce

3 cups frozen broccoli flowerets, thawed

3 large carrots, coarsely shredded (2 cups)

1 can (14 1/2 ounces) diced tomatoes, well drained

2 medium bell peppers, cut into 1/2-inch pieces

1 container (15 ounces) reduced-fat ricotta cheese

1/2 cup grated Parmesan cheese

1 large egg

3 1/2 cups shredded part-skim mozzarella cheese (14 ounces)

Cook and drain noodles as directed on package. Prepare Béchamel Sauce as directed.

Cut broccoli flowerets into bite-size pieces if necessary. Mix broccoli, carrots, tomatoes and bell peppers in large bowl. Mix ricotta cheese, Parmesan cheese and egg in small bowl.

Heat oven to 350°. Spoon 1 cup sauce in ungreased rectangular pan, 13 × 9 × 2 inches. Place 4 noodles over sauce. Spread half of cheese mixture, one-third of the vegetable mixture and 1 cup of sauce over noodles. Sprinkle with 1 cup of the mozzarella cheese. Top with 4 noodles; spread with remaining cheese mixture, one-third of vegetable mixture and 1 cup of sauce. Sprinkle with 1 cup mozzarella cheese. Top with remaining 4 noodles and vegetable mixture. Pour remaining sauce evenly over the top. Sprinkle with remaining 1 1/2 cups mozzarella cheese.

Bake uncovered 30 minutes; uncover and bake 30 minutes or until bubbly and hot in center. Let stand 15 minutes before cutting.

1 Serving: Calories 475 (Calories from Fat 180); Fat 20g (Saturated 10g); Cholesterol 75mg; Sodium 830mg; Carbohydrate 46g (Dietary Fiber 4g); Protein 32g.

BEAN LASAGNA

8 SERVINGS

Tomato Cream Sauce (page 143)

1 package (8 ounces) lasagna noodles

1 can (15 ounces) black beans, rinsed and drained

1 can (15 to 16 ounces) navy beans, rinsed and drained

2 cups small curd creamed cottage cheese

1 cup shredded mozzarella cheese (4 ounces)

2 tablespoons grated Romano or Parmesan cheese

1 tablespoon chopped fresh parsley

Heat oven to 375°. Grease rectangular baking dish, 12 × 8 × 2 inches. Prepare Tomato Cream Sauce. Cook and drain noodles as directed on package. Rinse with cold water; drain. Stir beans into sauce.

Place half of the noodles in baking dish. Spread half of the sauce over noodles. Spread half of the cottage cheese over sauce. Sprinkle with half of the mozzarella cheese. Top with remaining noodles, sauce, cottage cheese and mozzarella cheese. Sprinkle with Romano cheese and parsley.

Bake uncovered 35 to 45 minutes or until hot and bubbly. Let stand 5 minutes before cutting.

1 Serving: Calories 355 (Calories from Fat 65); Fat 7g (Saturated 4g); Cholesterol 20mg; Sodium 780mg; Carbohydrate 57g (Dietary Fiber 9g); Protein 25g.

Lasagna Primavera

RIGATONI WITH ARTICHOKES

6 SERVINGS

2 cups uncooked rigatoni pasta (6 ounces)

2 tablespoons margarine, butter or spread

1 1/2 cups soft bread crumbs (about 2 1/2 slices bread)

1 tablespoon chopped fresh parsley

1 teaspoon olive or vegetable oil

2 cloves garlic, finely chopped

3/4 cup chicken broth

2 tablespoons finely chopped oil-packed sun-dried tomatoes, drained

1 teaspoon cornstarch

1/4 teaspoon salt

1/4 teaspoon crushed red pepper

1/4 teaspoon pepper

1 can (14 ounces) artichokes hearts, drained

1 tablespoon grated Romano or Parmesan cheese

Cook and drain pasta as directed on package. Melt margarine in 10-inch skillet over medium-high heat. Cook bread crumbs in margarine 5 to 6 minutes, stirring occasionally, until light brown. Stir in parsley. Remove bread crumbs from skillet; keep warm.

Heat oil in same skillet over medium-high heat. Cook garlic in oil, stirring frequently, until golden.

Shake broth, tomatoes, cornstarch, salt, red pepper and pepper in tightly covered container. Gradually stir into garlic. Heat to boiling, stirring constantly. Boil and stir 1 minute. Stir in artichokes. Toss with pasta. Sprinkle with bread crumbs and cheese.

1 Serving: Calories 210 (Calories from Fat 55); Fat 6g (Saturated 1g); Cholesterol 0mg; Sodium 380mg; Carbohydrate 35g (Dietary Fiber 3g); Protein 7g.

SAUTÉED NOODLES AND VEGETABLES

4 SERVINGS

6 ounces uncooked somen noodles or whole wheat spaghetti

1/4 cup dry sherry or chicken broth

1 teaspoon vegetable oil

4 ounces sliced mushrooms (1 1/2 cups)

3 medium carrots, shredded (1 1/2 cups)

1 small onion, chopped (1/4 cup)

1 tablespoon finely chopped gingerroot

3 cups thinly sliced napa (Chinese) cabbage (12 ounces)

3 tablespoons soy sauce

1 teaspoon sesame oil

Break noodles into 3-inch pieces. Cook and drain noodles as directed on package.

Heat sherry and vegetable oil in 12-inch skillet over medium-high heat. Cook mushrooms, carrots, onion and gingerroot in oil mixture, stirring frequently, until mushrooms are tender. Stir in cabbage. Cook, stirring frequently, until crisp-tender. Stir in soy sauce, sesame oil and noodles; cook until hot.

1 Serving: Calories 170 (Calories from Fat 25); Fat 3g (Saturated 1g); Cholesterol 0mg; Sodium 830mg; Carbohydrate 35g (Dietary Fiber 3g); Protein 4g.

Chili Cheese Macaroni Casserole

5 servings

1 package (7 ounces) elbow macaroni (2 cups)

1 can (4 ounces) chopped green chilies, drained

1 1/2 cups shredded Cheddar cheese (6 ounces)

1 cup sour cream

1 small onion, finely chopped (1/4 cup)

1/2 teaspoon salt

1/2 teaspoon dried oregano leaves

4 slices bacon, crisply cooked and crumbled

1/2 cup crushed tortilla chips (any flavor)

Heat oven to 350°. Cook and drain macaroni as directed on package. Mix macaroni, chilies, 3/4 cup of the cheese, the sour cream, onion, salt and oregano in ungreased 2-quart casserole.

Mix bacon, tortilla chips and remaining cheese. Sprinkle over macaroni mixture. Bake uncovered 25 to 30 minutes or until hot and bubbly.

1 Serving: Calories 430 (Calories from Fat 215); Fat 24g (Saturated 14g); Cholesterol 70mg; Sodium 780mg; Carbohydrate 37g (Dietary Fiber 1g); Protein 17g.

Tortellini and Cheese

4 servings

1 package (9 ounces) refrigerated cheese-filled tortellini

2 tablespoons margarine, butter or spread

2 small zucchini, cut lengthwise in half, then cut crosswise into 1/2-inch slices

1 large onion, chopped (1 cup)

2 tablespoons all-purpose flour

1 tablespoon chopped fresh or 3/4 teaspoon dried dill weed

1/4 teaspoon salt

1/4 teaspoon pepper

1 1/2 cups milk

1 cup shredded Swiss cheese (4 ounces)

Cook and drain tortellini as directed on package. Melt margarine in 10-inch skillet over medium-high heat. Cook zucchini and onion in margarine, stirring occasionally, until zucchini is crisp-tender; reduce heat to medium.

Stir in flour, dill weed, salt and pepper. Cook, stirring constantly, until bubbly; remove from heat. Stir in milk. Heat to boiling, stirring constantly. Boil and stir 1 minute. Stir in cheese until melted. Fold in tortellini; cook until hot.

1 Serving: Calories 360 (Calories from Fat 170); Fat 19g (Saturated 8g); Cholesterol 90mg; Sodium 600mg; Carbohydrate 28g (Dietary Fiber 2g); Protein 21g.

LEMON-CHIVE PASTA AND PEPPERS

4 SERVINGS

1/4 cup margarine, butter or spread

1 small red bell pepper, cut into thin strips

1 small green bell pepper, cut into thin strips

1 teaspoon grated lemon peel

1 tablespoon chopped fresh chives

1/2 teaspoon salt

1/8 teaspoon pepper

Dash of ground nutmeg

2 tablespoons lemon juice

4 cups hot cooked pasta (any variety)

Melt margarine in 10-inch skillet over medium-high heat. Cook bell peppers, lemon peel, chives, salt, pepper and nutmeg in margarine, stirring occasionally, until bell peppers are crisp-tender. Stir in lemon juice; cook until hot. Serve over pasta.

1 Serving: Calories 295 (Calories from Fat 110); Fat 12g (Saturated 3g); Cholesterol 0mg; Sodium 400mg; Carbohydrate 42g (Dietary Fiber 2g); Protein 7g.

MAFALDE WITH CREAMY ROASTED GARLIC

5 SERVINGS

Roasting the garlic gives it a rich and mellow flavor.

2 bulbs garlic (about 2 ounces each)

3 cups uncooked mafalde (mini-lasagna noodle) pasta (6 ounces)

1/2 cup half-and-half

1 tablespoon balsamic vinegar

1/2 teaspoon salt

1/4 teaspoon pepper

1 small red bell pepper, chopped (1/2 cup)

2 tablespoons chopped fresh parsley

Heat oven to 350°. Roast garlic as directed on page 97. Cook and drain pasta as directed on package. Remove garlic from bulbs by squeezing from the bottom.

Mix garlic, half-and-half, vinegar, salt and pepper in 1-quart saucepan. Cook over very low heat just until heated through. Stir in bell pepper and parsley. Toss sauce with pasta.

1 Serving: Calories 230 (Calories from Fat 35); Fat 4g (Saturated 2g); Cholesterol 10mg; Sodium 230mg; Carbohydrate 43g (Dietary Fiber 2g); Protein 8g.

Mafalde with Creamy Roasted Garlic

MACARONI AND CHEESE

4 SERVINGS

1 package (7 ounces) elbow macaroni (2 cups)

1/4 cup margarine, butter or spread

1/4 cup all-purpose flour

1/2 teaspoon salt

1/4 teaspoon pepper

1/4 teaspoon ground mustard (dry)

1/4 teaspoon Worcestershire sauce

2 cups milk

2 cups grated or cubed sharp Cheddar cheese (8 ounces)

Heat oven to 350°. Grease 2-quart casserole. Cook and drain macaroni as directed on package. Melt margarine in 3-quart saucepan over medium heat. Stir in flour, salt, pepper, mustard and Worcestershire sauce. Cook, stirring constantly, until mixture is smooth and bubbly. Gradually stir in milk. Heat to boiling, stirring constantly. Boil and stir 1 minute.

Stir in cheese until melted. Stir in macaroni until well coated. Spoon into casserole. Bake uncovered 20 to 25 minutes or until golden brown.

1 Serving: Calories 605 (Calories from Fat 305); Fat 34g (Saturated 16g); Cholesterol 70mg; Sodium 820mg; Carbohydrate 51g (Dietary Fiber 1g); Protein 25g.

CURRIED PASTA WITH SPINACH

4 SERVINGS

1 package (9 ounces) refrigerated cheese-filled ravioli

1 package (10 ounces) frozen chopped spinach

1/4 cup cream cheese (2 ounces), softened

2/3 cup canned coconut milk

1/3 cup chicken broth

3/4 teaspoon curry powder

1/4 teaspoon salt

1/3 cup sliced green onions (4 medium)

1/4 cup chopped peanuts

Cook and drain ravioli as directed on package. Cook and drain spinach as directed on package.

Mix cream cheese, coconut milk, broth, curry powder and salt in 1-quart saucepan. Cook, stirring occasionally, until hot. Spoon spinach onto serving plate. Top with ravioli and sauce. Sprinkle with onions and peanuts.

1 Serving: Calories 290 (Calories from Fat 200); Fat 22g (Saturated 13g); Cholesterol 55mg; Sodium 670mg; Carbohydrate 15g (Dietary Fiber 2g); Protein 10g.

RATATOUILLE WITH DITALI

6 SERVINGS

1 tablespoon olive or vegetable oil

1 medium onion, chopped (1/2 cup)

1 clove garlic, finely chopped

1 cup uncooked ditali pasta (4 ounces)

1/2 teaspoon dried basil leaves

1/2 teaspoon dried oregano leaves

1/2 teaspoon salt

1/4 teaspoon pepper

2 small zucchini, cubed

1 small eggplant (1 pound), cubed

1 small green bell pepper, chopped (1/2 cup)

1 can (15 ounces) Italian-style stewed tomatoes, undrained

1 can (8 ounces) tomato sauce

Heat oil in Dutch oven over medium heat. Cook onion and garlic in oil, stirring occasionally, until onion is crisp-tender.

Stir in remaining ingredients. Heat to boiling; reduce heat to low. Simmer uncovered 10 to 15 minutes, stirring occasionally, until pasta and vegetables are tender.

1 Serving: Calories 155 (Calories from Fat 25); Fat 3g (Saturated 0g); Cholesterol 0mg; Sodium 530mg; Carbohydrate 31g (Dietary Fiber 4g); Protein 5g.

PESTO FRITTATA

6 SERVINGS

Cut into small wedges, this frittata also makes a great appetizer!

1/4 cup Basil Pesto (page 142)

6 ounces uncooked linguine

3/4 cup shredded provolone or mozzarella cheese (3 ounces)

5 eggs

1/2 teaspoon salt

3 roma (plum) tomatoes, sliced

Heat oven to 375°. Grease 10-inch pie plate. Prepare Basil Pesto. Cook and drain linguine as directed on package. Place in pie plate; press down slightly. Cool 5 minutes. Sprinkle with cheese.

Beat eggs, pesto and salt; pour over linguine and cheese. Arrange tomatoes on top. Bake 25 to 30 minutes or until center is set. Let stand 10 minutes before cutting. Serve with freshly ground pepper or crushed red pepper if desired.

1 Serving: Calories 260 (Calories from Fat 110); Fat 12g (Saturated 4g); Cholesterol 190mg; Sodium 460mg; Carbohydrate 26g (Dietary Fiber 1g); Protein 13g.

TOMATO CREAM PESTO PASTA

6 SERVINGS

This dish is a pretty presentation in pink and green! For added appeal, arrange pasta on an elegant platter, and garnish with fresh basil.

3/4 cup Basil Pesto (page 142)

12 ounces uncooked vermicelli

1 can (14 1/2 ounces) diced tomatoes, undrained

1/2 teaspoon dried basil leaves

1/2 cup evaporated milk

Prepare Basil Pesto. Cook and drain vermicelli as directed on package. Mix tomatoes and basil in 2-quart saucepan. Cook over medium-high heat 6 to 8 minutes, stirring occasionally, until most of liquid has evaporated; reduce heat to low. Stir in milk. Cook 1 minute, stirring occasionally.

Toss vermicelli with pesto until well coated. Spoon tomato sauce over vermicelli mixture.

1 Serving: Calories 350 (Calories from Fat 110); Fat 12g (Saturated 2g); Cholesterol 5mg; Sodium 410mg; Carbohydrate 52g (Dietary Fiber 3g); Protein 11g.

SWISS CAPELLINI TART

6 SERVINGS

Try serving this attractive tart for brunch with your favorite fresh fruit.

1 cup Béchamel Sauce (page 143)

4 ounces uncooked capellini (angel hair) pasta

18 slices French bread, about 1/4 inch thick

2 tablespoons margarine, butter or spread, softened

3/4 cup shredded Swiss cheese (3 ounces)

2 tablespoons chopped fresh or 2 teaspoons dried basil leaves

3 roma (plum) tomatoes, chopped (1 cup)

1/4 cup sliced green onions (3 medium)

2 tablespoons grated Romano or Parmesan cheese

Heat oven to 400°. Prepare Béchamel Sauce. Cook and drain pasta as directed on package.

Brush bread with margarine. Line bottom and side of 10-inch pie plate, 10 × 1 1/2 inches, with bread, slightly overlapping slices. Bake about 10 minutes or until light brown.

Reduce oven temperature to 350°. Stir Swiss cheese and 1 tablespoon of the basil into sauce. Toss sauce and pasta. Spoon into baked crust.

Mix tomatoes, onions and remaining 1 tablespoon basil. Sprinkle over pasta mixture; lightly press into surface. Sprinkle with Romano cheese. Bake 15 to 20 minutes or until heated through. Let stand 5 minutes before cutting.

1 Serving: Calories 330 (Calories from Fat 110); Fat 12g (Saturated 4g); Cholesterol 15mg; Sodium 510mg; Carbohydrate 45g (Dietary Fiber 2g); Protein 13g.

COUSCOUS PATTIES WITH CITRUS SAUCE

4 SERVINGS (2 PATTIES EACH)

Couscous seems more like a grain than pasta because of its small size. It is quick and easy to prepare and is complemented by almost any seasoning.

1 cup water

2/3 cup uncooked couscous

1/2 teaspoon salt

1/4 teaspoon pepper

1 teaspoon margarine, butter or spread

1 medium stalk celery, finely chopped
    (1/2 cup)

1 small onion, finely chopped (1/4 cup)

1 small carrot, shredded (1/3 cup)

2 cloves garlic, finely chopped

1 cup fine soft bread crumbs
    (about 1 1/2 slices bread)

1/3 cup sliced almonds, toasted

1 tablespoon chopped fresh chives

1 egg

1 egg yolk

Citrus Sauce (below)

2 tablespoons vegetable oil

Grease cookie sheet. Heat water to boiling in 1-quart saucepan. Stir in couscous, salt and pepper; remove from heat. Cover and let stand 5 minutes.

Melt margarine in 8-inch skillet over medium heat. Cook celery, onion, carrot and garlic in margarine, stirring occasionally, until vegetables are tender.

Mix couscous, vegetables, bread crumbs, almonds, chives, egg and egg yolk. Shape mixture into 8 patties, about 1/2 inch thick. Place on cookie sheet. Cover and refrigerate at least 1 hour but no longer than 24 hours.

Prepare Citrus Sauce. Heat oil in 10-inch skillet over medium heat. Cook patties in oil about 8 minutes, turning once, until golden brown. Serve with sauce.

CITRUS SAUCE

2 teaspoons cornstarch

1 teaspoon sugar

1/8 teaspoon salt

3/4 cup orange juice

1 tablespoon lemon juice

1 teaspoon grated orange peel

2 tablespoons currants or raisins

1 1/2 teaspoons chopped fresh chives

Mix cornstarch, sugar and salt in 1-quart saucepan. Gradually stir in juices and orange peel. Bring to a boil, stirring constantly, until thickened. Stir in currants and chives.

1 Serving: Calories 350 (Calories from Fat 145); Fat 16g (Saturated 3g); Cholesterol 105mg; Sodium 440mg; Carbohydrate 45g (Dietary Fiber 3g); Protein 9g.

QUICK VEGETABLE TIP

The next time you're making a recipe that combines pasta and vegetables into one mixture, try our tip that saves both time and an extra saucepan.

While the pasta is boiling, add vegetables to the boiling pasta water during the last 5 to 10 minutes of cooking. Some vegetables will take a short time to cook and others longer. Drain the pasta and vegetables and continue with the recipe. It's that simple, that easy, that quick!

Couscous Patties with Citrus Sauce

Red Beans with Orzo

8 SERVINGS

1 can (14 1/2 ounces) vegetable broth

3/4 cup uncooked rosamarina (orzo) pasta (4 1/2 ounces)

1 can (15 to 16 ounces) kidney beans, rinsed and drained

2 teaspoons chili powder

1/2 teaspoon ground cumin

1 tablespoon olive or vegetable oil

1 medium onion, chopped (1/2 cup)

1 clove garlic, finely chopped

3 cups broccoli flowerets

1 small yellow bell pepper, cut into 1-inch pieces

2 tablespoons water

1/4 teaspoon salt

1 small carrot, shredded (1/3 cup)

Heat broth to boiling in 3-quart saucepan. Stir in pasta, beans, chili powder and cumin; reduce heat to low. Cover and simmer 25 to 30 minutes, stirring occasionally, until liquid is absorbed.

Heat oil in 10-inch skillet over medium heat. Cook onion and garlic in oil, stirring occasionally, until onion is tender. Stir in broccoli, bell pepper, water and salt. Heat to boiling; reduce heat to low. Cover and simmer 3 to 4 minutes or until vegetables are crisp-tender; drain if necessary.

Spoon pasta mixture onto serving platter. Top with vegetables. Sprinkle with carrot.

1 Serving: Calories 170 (Calories from Fat 35); Fat 4g (Saturated 1g); Cholesterol 10mg; Sodium 370mg; Carbohydrate 28g (Dietary Fiber 5g); Protein 10g.

Spicy Noodle Soup

6 SERVINGS

3 cans (14 1/2 ounces each) ready-to-serve vegetable broth

1 jar (16 ounces) salsa

1 can (15 ounces) black beans, rinsed and drained

1 can (11 ounces) vacuum-packed whole kernel corn, drained

1 package (5 ounces) Japanese curly noodles

1/3 cup chopped fresh cilantro or parsley

1 tablespoon lime juice

1 teaspoon chili powder

1/4 teaspoon ground cumin

1/4 teaspoon pepper

2 tablespoons grated Parmesan cheese

Heat broth to boiling in Dutch oven. Stir in remaining ingredients except cheese; reduce heat to medium. Cook 5 to 6 minutes, stirring occasionally, until noodles are tender. Sprinkle with cheese.

1 Serving: Calories 345 (Calories from Fat 65); Fat 7g (Saturated 2g); Cholesterol 40mg; Sodium 1240mg; Carbohydrate 58g (Dietary Fiber 10g); Protein 23g.

CURLY MINESTRONE

6 SERVINGS

1 tablespoon olive or vegetable oil

1 medium onion, chopped (1/2 cup)

1 medium stalk celery, sliced (1/2 cup)

1 clove garlic, finely chopped

2 cups frozen broccoli, cauliflower, water
    chestnuts and red bell pepper

1 cup uncooked fusilli pasta (3 ounces)

1/4 cup chopped fresh parsley or
    4 teaspoons dried parsley flakes

1 teaspoon dried basil leaves

1/2 teaspoon dried oregano leaves

1/2 teaspoon salt

1/4 teaspoon pepper

3 cans (14 1/2 ounces each) vegetable broth

1 can (15 ounces) Italian-style stewed
    tomatoes, undrained

1 can (15 to 16 ounces) garbanzo beans,
    rinsed and drained

1/4 cup grated Romano or Parmesan cheese

Heat oil in Dutch oven over medium-high heat. Cook onion, celery and garlic in oil, stirring occasionally, until crisp-tender. Stir in remaining ingredients except cheese. Heat to boiling; reduce heat to medium.

Cook uncovered 10 to 12 minutes, stirring occasionally, until pasta is tender. Sprinkle each serving with cheese.

1 Serving: Calories 390 (Calories from Fat 90); Fat 10g (Saturated 3g); Cholesterol 45mg; Sodium 1010mg; Carbohydrate 57g (Dietary Fiber 9g); Protein 27g.

JUST A PINCH OF SUGAR!

Whether to add sugar to cooked tomato-based sauces can spark quite a debate! There are those who say sugar should never be added to a tomato sauce and there are others who add sugar to cut acidic or bitter flavors, or because they like a sweeter tasting sauce.

If a tomato or spaghetti sauce tastes a little too acidic, bitter or harsh, a little bit of sugar can mellow the sauce and remove the unwanted flavors. To add sugar to a tomato or spaghetti sauce, start with a small amount, such as 1/2 teaspoon sugar for each 1 1/2 to 2 cups of sauce. Stir sugar into the sauce and allow it to simmer several minutes before tasting. Keep adding sugar in 1/2-teaspoon amounts until the sauce suits your taste. Either white or brown sugar can be used.

In the end, whether or not you make a sauce with sugar is between you and your taste buds!

GARDEN PASTA AND BEANS

6 SERVINGS

3/4 cup uncooked small pasta shells
(3 ounces)

1 tablespoon olive or vegetable oil

2 small zucchini, thinly sliced (1 cup)

1 medium onion, chopped (1/2 cup)

1/4 cup chopped celery

1/4 cup chopped green bell pepper

1 clove garlic, finely chopped

1 can (15 ounces) Italian-style tomatoes,
undrained

3/4 teaspoon Italian seasoning

1 can (15 to 16 ounces) cannellini beans,
rinsed and drained

2 tablespoons grated Parmesan cheese

Cook and drain pasta as directed on package. Heat oil in 3-quart saucepan over medium-high heat. Cook zucchini, onion, celery, bell pepper and garlic in oil, stirring occasionally, until tender.

Stir in tomatoes and Italian seasoning, breaking up tomatoes. Heat to boiling; reduce heat to low. Simmer uncovered 10 minutes, stirring occasionally. Stir in beans and pasta; cook until hot. Sprinkle with cheese.

1 Serving: Calories 225 (Calories from Fat 45); Fat 5g (Saturated 1g); Cholesterol 0mg; Sodium 350mg; Carbohydrate 40g (Dietary Fiber 6g); Protein 11g.

6

SALADS

Black Bean-Chicken Salad with
Creamy Cilantro Pesto Dressing (p.166)

ORIENTAL CHICKEN MANICOTTI SALAD

4 SERVINGS

This is an Italian interpretation of a classic Chinese chicken salad. Purchased coleslaw mix makes this salad quick to prepare.

Tangy Peanut Dressing (below)

8 uncooked manicotti shells

5 cups coleslaw mix

1 1/2 cups finely chopped cooked chicken breast

1 cup fresh bean sprouts, finely chopped

1/2 cup peanuts, chopped

1/4 cup canned water chestnuts, chopped

Prepare Tangy Peanut Dressing. Cook and drain manicotti as directed on package. Rinse with cold water; drain. Finely chop 1 cup of the coleslaw mix. Mix finely chopped coleslaw, the chicken, bean sprouts, peanuts and water chestnuts.

Fill manicotti with chicken mixture. Divide remaining coleslaw mix among serving plates. Top with manicotti. Drizzle with dressing.

TANGY PEANUT DRESSING

1/3 cup vegetable oil

2 tablespoons rice wine or white vinegar

2 tablespoons creamy peanut butter

1 tablespoon soy sauce

1/8 teaspoon ground red pepper (cayenne)

1 clove garlic, finely chopped

Mix all ingredients using wire whisk.

1 Serving: Calories 540 (Calories from Fat 295); Fat 33g (Saturated 5g); Cholesterol 40mg; Sodium 350mg; Carbohydrate 38g (Dietary Fiber 5g); Protein 28g.

Pasta Salad Pointers

One look at deli counters, gourmet take-outs and restaurant menus shows how immensely popular cold pasta salads have become. Infinite combinations offering a wide variety of color, flavor and texture are possible with a little imagination. By far, the easiest pasta salads to make combine your favorite ingredients such as meat, cheese and vegetables with bottled salad dressing, which adds instant flavor. As simple as making pasta salads may seem, following the suggestions below will ensure successful salads!

1. When preparing the pasta for cold pasta salads, it is important to rinse the pasta with cold water and drain. This not only cools the pasta right away, but removes excess starch that can cause cold pasta salads to absorb too much of the dressing and become dry.

2. If cooking pasta that won't be used the same day, toss the pasta with a small amount of the same dressing the recipe uses or oil, to prevent it from sticking.

3. Many cold pasta salads become more flavorful if they have been refrigerated for several hours. Recipes that are robust in flavor can generally be eaten immediately. The pasta salad recipes in this book indicate whether or not they need refrigeration time to blend flavors.

Oriental Chicken Manicotti Salad

BLACK BEAN-CHICKEN SALAD WITH CREAMY CILANTRO PESTO DRESSING

6 SERVINGS

Cilantro is similar to parsley, but the flavor is much more pungent, making a flavorful pesto. Cilantro is now readily available in the produce section of your grocery store year-round.

Creamy Cilantro Pesto Dressing (right)

2 teaspoons olive or vegetable oil

1 pound boneless, skinless chicken breast halves, cut into 1/2-inch strips

1 teaspoon chili powder

1/4 teaspoon garlic salt

2 cups uncooked rigatoni pasta (6 ounces)

1 large tomato, chopped (1 cup)

1 can (15 ounces) black beans, rinsed and drained

Prepare Creamy Cilantro Pesto Dressing. Heat oil in 10-inch skillet over medium-high heat. Cook chicken in oil 6 to 8 minutes, stirring occasionally, until no longer pink in center. Toss chicken, chili powder and garlic salt; set aside.

Cook and drain pasta as directed on package. Rinse with cold water; drain. Mix pasta, chicken, dressing, tomato and beans.

CREAMY CILANTRO PESTO DRESSING

1 1/2 cups chopped fresh cilantro

1/2 cup shredded Parmesan cheese

1/3 cup pine nuts

1/3 cup olive or vegetable oil

1/4 cup whipping (heavy) cream

1 teaspoon grated lemon peel

1 tablespoon lemon juice

1/8 teaspoon ground red pepper (cayenne)

2 cloves garlic

Place all ingredients in food processor or blender. Cover and process until smooth.

1 Serving: Calories 545 (Calories from Fat 235); Fat 26g (Saturated 6g); Cholesterol 60mg; Sodium 370mg; Carbohydrate 54g (Dietary Fiber 7g); Protein 31g.

TURKEY CLUB PASTA SALAD WITH LEMON-BASIL DRESSING

6 SERVINGS

For a quick meal, try this contemporary salad version of the classic sandwich.

Lemon-Basil Dressing (right)

1 package (7 ounces) small pasta shells

1 1/2 cups fully cooked smoked turkey, cut into 1×1/4-inch strips

1 1/2 cups shredded lettuce

1 cup shredded Swiss cheese (4 ounces)

1 large tomato, chopped (1 cup)

6 slices bacon, crisply cooked and crumbled

Prepare Lemon-Basil Dressing. Cook and drain pasta as directed on package. Rinse with cold water; drain.

Mix pasta, dressing and remaining ingredients in large bowl. Cover and refrigerate 1 to 2 hours to blend flavors.

LEMON-BASIL DRESSING

3/4 cup mayonnaise or salad dressing

2 tablespoons chopped fresh or 1 teaspoon dried basil leaves

1 teaspoon grated lemon peel

1 teaspoon lemon juice

Mix all ingredients.

1 Serving: Calories 490 (Calories from Fat 290); Fat 32g (Saturated 8g); Cholesterol 65mg; Sodium 330mg; Carbohydrate 29g (Dietary Fiber 1g); Protein 23g.

TOMATO-BASIL PASTA SALAD WITH AIOLI DRESSING

6 SERVINGS

This is for garlic lovers! Aioli is a popular, strongly flavored garlic mayonnaise that originated in southern France.

Aioli Dressing (right)

3 cups uncooked mafalde (mini-lasagna noodle) pasta (6 ounces)

2 large tomatoes, chopped (2 cups)

1/2 cup chopped fresh basil leaves

4 ounces prosciutto or fully cooked smoked ham, cut into 2×1/2-inch strips

1/2 cup shredded Parmesan cheese

Prepare Aioli Dressing. Cook and drain pasta as directed on package. Rinse with cold water; drain.

Mix pasta and dressing in large bowl. Fold in tomatoes, basil and prosciutto. Cover and refrigerate 1 hour to blend flavors. Sprinkle with cheese just before serving.

AIOLI DRESSING

3 cloves garlic, finely chopped

1/2 cup mayonnaise or salad dressing

Mix all ingredients.

1 Serving: Calories 450 (Calories from Fat 180); Fat 20g (Saturated 4g); Cholesterol 25mg; Sodium 380mg; Carbohydrate 55g (Dietary Fiber 2g); Protein 15g.

GARDEN PATCH PASTA SALAD

8 SERVINGS

Ideal for the busy cook, this side salad can be made in a jiffy and can also be prepared ahead.

1 1/2 cups uncooked ditali pasta (6 ounces)

1 cup sliced mushrooms (3 ounces)

1 cup cubed Colby or Cheddar cheese

3/4 cup ranch dressing

1 small red bell pepper, chopped (1/2 cup)

1 package (16 ounces) frozen French-style green beans, thawed

3/4 cup canned French fried onions

Cook and drain pasta as directed on package. Rinse with cold water; drain.

Mix pasta and remaining ingredients except onions in large bowl. Sprinkle each serving with onions.

1 Serving: Calories 270 (Calories from Fat 145); Fat 16g (Saturated 5g); Cholesterol 20mg; Sodium 310mg; Carbohydrate 26g (Dietary Fiber 2g); Protein 8g.

SHRIMP PASTA SALAD WITH FRESH FRUIT SALSA

6 SERVINGS

Looking for a light and refreshing salad? Try this intriguing combination with either fresh or frozen cooked shrimp.

Fresh Fruit Salsa (below)

2 cups uncooked farfalle (bow tie) pasta (4 ounces)

1 head Boston lettuce

1 medium cucumber, cut lengthwise in half, then sliced crosswise

12 ounces cooked (peeled and deveined) large shrimp

1 avocado, sliced

Prepare Fresh Fruit Salsa. Cook and drain pasta as directed on package. Rinse with cold water; drain.

Divide lettuce leaves among serving plates. Arrange pasta, cucumber, shrimp and avocado on lettuce-lined plates. Serve with salsa.

FRESH FRUIT SALSA

1/2 cup coarsely chopped pineapple

1/2 cup coarsely chopped strawberries

1 teaspoon grated orange peel

2 tablespoons orange juice

1 tablespoon olive or vegetable oil

1/4 teaspoon salt

1/8 teaspoon white pepper

2 kiwifruit, peeled and coarsely chopped

1 small jalapeño chile, chopped

Mix all ingredients.

1 Serving: Calories 230 (Calories from Fat 70); Fat 8g (Saturated 1g); Cholesterol 110mg; Sodium 220mg; Carbohydrate 26g (Dietary Fiber 3g); Protein 16g.

Shrimp Pasta Salad with Fresh Fruit Salsa

EAST INDIAN CURRIED PASTA SALAD

4 SERVINGS

The spices here make the salad an Indian treat!

4 ounces uncooked capellini (angel hair) pasta, broken into thirds

2 cups cooked cubed chicken

1 1/2 cups frozen green peas, thawed

1 large tomato, chopped (1 cup)

1/2 cup raisins

3/4 cup mayonnaise or salad dressing

1/2 cup plain yogurt

1 1/2 teaspoons curry powder

1/2 teaspoon ground allspice

1/2 teaspoon ground cumin

1/4 teaspoon ground ginger

1/4 teaspoon salt

1/4 cup sliced almonds

1/4 cup coconut, toasted

Cook and drain pasta as directed on package. Rinse with cold water; drain.

Mix pasta, chicken, peas, tomato and raisins in large glass or plastic bowl. Mix mayonnaise, yogurt, curry powder, allspice, cumin and ginger and salt; stir into pasta mixture. Cover and refrigerate 1 to 2 hours to blend flavors. Sprinkle with almonds and coconut just before serving.

1 Serving: Calories 715 (Calories from Fat 395); Fat 44g (Saturated 8g); Cholesterol 85mg; Sodium 510mg; Carbohydrate 54g (Dietary Fiber 5g); Protein 31g.

ITALIAN TUNA PASTA SALAD

6 SERVINGS

Sun-dried Tomato Pesto Dressing (below)

2 cups uncooked medium pasta shells (5 ounces)

1 cup frozen cut green beans, thawed

1/4 cup chopped fresh parsley

1 can (15 to 16 ounces) cannellini beans, rinsed and drained

1 can (6 1/8 ounces) tuna packed in water, drained

Prepare Sun-dried Tomato Pesto Dressing. Cook and drain pasta as directed on package. Rinse with cold water; drain.

Toss pasta, dressing and remaining ingredients in large glass or plastic bowl. Serve immediately, or cover and refrigerate up to 24 hours.

SUN-DRIED TOMATO PESTO DRESSING

3 tablespoons sun-dried oil-packed tomatoes, drained

2 tablespoons chopped fresh or 2 teaspoons dried basil leaves

1 tablespoon pine nuts

1 tablespoon shredded Parmesan cheese

1/4 cup olive or vegetable oil

2 tablespoons lemon juice

1 clove garlic

Place all ingredients in food processor or blender. Cover and process until well blended.

1 Serving: Calories 385 (Calories from Fat 115); Fat 13g (Saturated 2g); Cholesterol 10mg; Sodium 270mg; Carbohydrate 53g (Dietary Fiber 5g); Protein 19g.

MIDWEST GRILLED STEAK SALAD WITH CREAMY HERB CHEESE DRESSING

4 SERVINGS

You'll love this light, refreshing twist on a typical midwestern steak dinner!

Creamy Herb Cheese Dressing (right)

3/4 pound beef boneless sirloin steak (about 3/4 inch thick)

Salt and pepper to taste, if desired

2 cups uncooked mostaccioli pasta (6 ounces)

1 cup cherry tomato halves

5 thin slices red onion

1 can (14 to 15 ounces) baby corn nuggets

Prepare Creamy Herb Cheese Dressing. Sprinkle beef with salt and pepper. Grill beef uncovered 4 to 5 inches from medium coals 12 to 16 minutes for medium doneness, turning once.* Cut beef into 2×1/4-inch strips.

Cook and drain pasta as directed on package. Rinse with cold water; drain. Toss pasta, beef, tomatoes, onion and corn in large bowl. Serve with dressing.

CREAMY HERB CHEESE DRESSING

4 ounces soft cream cheese with chives and onion

3 tablespoons milk

1 teaspoon Dijon mustard

Beat all ingredients with fork or wire whisk.

*Broiler Directions—Set oven control to broil. Broil beef with top 2 to 3 inches from heat 15 to 17 minutes for medium doneness, turning once.

1 Serving: Calories 525 (Calories from Fat 135); Fat 15g (Saturated 8g); Cholesterol 70mg; Sodium 440mg; Carbohydrate 72g (Dietary Fiber 4g); Protein 29g.

THREE-CHEESE AND HAM PASTA SALAD

6 SERVINGS

This is a contemporary version of a classic pasta salad. Cheddar, Parmesan and blue cheeses blend together for great flavor in this easy salad.

2 cups uncooked radiatore (nugget) pasta (6 ounces)

2 cups shredded Cheddar cheese (8 ounces)

1 1/2 cups cubed fully cooked smoked ham

1 cup blue cheese dressing

1/2 cup shredded Parmesan cheese

1/3 cup sour cream

1/4 cup chopped green onions (3 medium)

1 can (11 ounces) whole kernel corn with red and green peppers, drained

Cook and drain pasta as directed on package. Rinse with cold water; drain.

Mix pasta and remaining ingredients in large bowl. Cover and refrigerate 2 hours to blend flavors.

1 Serving: Calories 670 (Calories from Fat 380); Fat 42g (Saturated 16g); Cholesterol 80mg; Sodium 1450mg; Carbohydrate 47g (Dietary Fiber 3g); Protein 29g.

BROCCOLI-WALNUT MOSTACCIOLI SALAD

4 SERVINGS

The unique flavor and color of this salad can be attributed to the balsamic vinegar. Balsamic is imported from Italy and has a full bodied, slightly sweet flavor and rich reddish brown color. Available in kitchen specialty shops and some large supermarkets, it is definitely worth the extra cost.

2 cups uncooked mostaccioli pasta (6 ounces)

1 envelope (0.75 ounce) herb-and-garlic sauce mix or 1 envelope (0.5 ounce) pesto sauce mix

1/4 cup olive or vegetable oil

1/4 cup balsamic or red wine vinegar

2 cups broccoli flowerets

1 cup chopped walnuts

1/2 cup sliced ripe olives

1/2 cup shredded Parmesan cheese

Cook and drain pasta as directed on package. Rinse with cold water; drain. Mix sauce mix, oil and vinegar.

Toss pasta, sauce mixture and remaining ingredients in large glass or plastic bowl. Cover and refrigerate at least 1 hour to blend flavors.

1 Serving: Calories 680 (Calories from Fat 350); Fat 39g (Saturated 6g); Cholesterol 10mg; Sodium 830mg; Carbohydrate 63g (Dietary Fiber 5g); Protein 19g.

Broccoli-Walnut Mostaccioli Salad

QUICK BREAD FIX-UPS

Imagine your favorite pasta meal with some warm, crusty bread—then imagine that bread with a fresh, delicious topping! Moving out of the plain old garlic bread routine is easy with these delectable recipes; all start with purchased bread with the addition of easy-to-find topping ingredients. Whether you want a bread for the whole family, casual entertaining or a fancy dinner party, these recipes are sure to be a hit!

ONION, CHEESE AND ALMOND FOCACCIA

16 WEDGES

1 Italian bread shell or purchased pizza crust (12 inches in diameter)

1/3 cup sweet honey mustard

2 tablespoons margarine, butter or spread

1 large onion, chopped (1 cup)

2 cups shredded smoked Cheddar or Gouda cheese (8 ounces)

1/2 cup sliced almonds

Heat oven to 375°. Place bread shell on ungreased cookie sheet. Spread with mustard. Melt margarine in 10-inch skillet over medium-high heat. Cook onion in margarine, stirring occasionally, until tender.

Spoon onion evenly onto bread shell. Sprinkle with cheese and almonds. Bake 15 to 20 minutes or until cheese is melted. Cut into 16 wedges.

2 Wedges: Calories 450 (Calories from Fat 180); Fat 20g (Saturated 8g); Cholesterol 30mg; Sodium 710mg; Carbohydrate 55g (Dietary Fiber 3g); Protein 16g.

French Onion Toasts

8 TOASTS

4 hamburger buns, split

1/3 cup mayonnaise or salad dressing

1 teaspoon onion soup mix (dry)

1/2 cup shredded mozzarella cheese (2 ounces)

1/4 cup grated Parmesan cheese

Set oven control to broil. Place buns, cut sides up, on ungreased cookie sheet. Broil with tops 4 to 6 inches from heat about 45 seconds or until lightly toasted.

Mix mayonnaise and soup mix; spread on buns. Sprinkle with cheeses. Broil 45 to 60 seconds or until cheese is melted.

1 Toast: Calories 155 (Calories from Fat 90); Fat 10g (Saturated 3g); Cholesterol 10mg; Sodium 280mg; Carbohydrate 11g (Dietary Fiber 0g); Protein 5g.

Olive Crostini

12 SLICES

12 slices French bread, 1 inch thick

1/3 cup chopped green olives

1/3 cup chopped ripe olives

1 container (5 ounces) garlic-and-herb or herb soft spreadable cheese

Set oven control to broil. Place bread on ungreased cookie sheet. Broil with tops 4 to 6 inches from heat 30 to 60 seconds or until lightly toasted.

Mix olives and cheese; spread on bread. Broil 1 to 2 minutes or until cheese is warm.

1 Slice: Calories 75 (Calories from Fat 35); Fat 4g (Saturated 2g); Cholesterol 10mg; Sodium 260mg; Carbohydrate 8g (Dietary Fiber 0g); Protein 2g.

(Continued on next page)

PARMESAN RANCH CHEESE TOASTS

8 TOASTS

4 frankfurter buns, split

1/4 cup ranch dressing

1/3 cup chopped green onions (4 medium)

1/4 cup grated Parmesan cheese

Set oven control to broil. Place buns, cut sides up, on ungreased cookie sheet. Spread with dressing. Sprinkle with onions and cheese.

Broil with tops 4 to 6 inches from heat about 1 minute or until topping begins to bubble.

1 Toast: Calories 105 (Calories from Fat 45); Fat 5g (Saturated 1g); Cholesterol 5mg; Sodium 230mg; Carbohydrate 12g (Dietary Fiber 0g); Protein 3g.

PESTO PARMESAN LOAF

16 SLICES

1 loaf (1 pound) French bread, cut horizontally in half

1/2 cup pesto

1/2 cup coarsely chopped oil-packed sun-dried tomatoes, drained, or 1/2 cup chopped fresh tomato

1 cup shredded mozzarella cheese (4 ounces)

Set oven control to broil. Place bread, cut sides up, on ungreased cookie sheet. Broil with tops 4 to 6 inches from heat about 1 minute or until lightly toasted.

Spread pesto on bread. Sprinkle with tomatoes and cheese. Broil 1 to 2 minutes or until cheese is melted.

2 Slices: Calories 290 (Calories from Fat 135); Fat 15g (Saturated 4g); Cholesterol 10mg; Sodium 480mg; Carbohydrate 31g (Dietary Fiber 2g); Protein 10g.

ARTICHOKE ROSEMARY BRUSCHETTA

12 SLICES

1 loaf (1 pound) French bread, cut
    horizontally in half

1 cup shredded mozzarella cheese
    (4 ounces)

1/2 cup grated Parmesan cheese

1 tablespoon chopped fresh or
    1 teaspoon dried rosemary
    leaves, crumbled

2/3 cup mayonnaise or salad dressing

1 jar (6 ounces) marinated artichoke
    hearts, drained and chopped

Heat oven to 375°. Place bread, cut sides up, on ungreased cookie sheet. Bake 10 minutes.

Mix 1/2 cup of the mozzarella cheese, the Parmesan cheese, rosemary, mayonnaise and artichokes; spread on bread. Sprinkle with remaining 1/2 cup mozzarella cheese. Bake 15 to 20 minutes or until cheese is melted.

1 Slice: Calories 240 (Calories from Fat 125); Fat 14g (Saturated 3g); Cholesterol 15mg; Sodium 440mg; Carbohydrate 21g (Dietary Fiber 1g); Protein 8g.

PASTA SALAD PRIMAVERA

4 MAIN-DISH OR **8** SIDE-DISH SERVINGS

For an especially colorful salad, use a combination of red, yellow, green and orange bell peppers. Serve this salad as a light meal or side dish with grilled chicken or fish.

1 package (9 ounces) refrigerated cheese-filled ravioli

2 cups cubed bell peppers

1 cup broccoli flowerets

1 cup sliced mushrooms (3 ounces)

1/3 cup sliced radishes

1/3 cup chopped cucumber

2 medium carrots, sliced (1 cup)

1 cup plain yogurt

1/2 cup sour cream

1/2 cup shredded Parmesan cheese

1 tablespoon chopped fresh or 1 teaspoon dried dill weed

1/4 teaspoon salt

Cook ravioli as directed on package; drain. Rinse with cold water; drain.

Mix ravioli, bell peppers, broccoli, mushrooms, radishes, cucumber and carrots in large bowl. Mix remaining ingredients; stir into ravioli mixture.

1 Serving: Calories 240 (Calories from Fat 100); Fat 11g (Saturated 7g); Cholesterol 35mg; Sodium 740mg; Carbohydrate 25g (Dietary Fiber 3g); Protein 13g.

TOSSED TORTELLINI SALAD

4 MAIN-DISH OR **6** SIDE-DISH SERVINGS

To save time, purchase ready-to-serve salad greens available in the produce section of the grocery store. Try the dressing suggested, or top the salad off with your favorite purchased dressing.

1 package (9 ounces) refrigerated cheese-filled tortellini

6 cups bite-size pieces mixed salad greens

1 cup sliced mushrooms (3 ounces)

1/2 cup smoked whole almonds

2 medium carrots, sliced (1 cup)

3/4 cup ranch dressing

Cook and drain tortellini as directed on package. Rinse with cold water; drain.

Toss tortellini and remaining ingredients except dressing in large serving dish. Serve with dressing.

1 Serving: Calories 420 (Calories from Fat 270); Fat 30g (Saturated 5g); Cholesterol 70mg; Sodium 800mg; Carbohydrate 27g (Dietary Fiber 4g); Protein 15g.

Tossed Tortellini Salad

MIXED BEAN PASTA SALAD

8 SERVINGS

A sweet and tangy dressing perks up the flavor of this bean trio. Guaranteed to be a picnic or potluck favorite!

1 1/3 cups uncooked rotini pasta (4 1/4 ounces)

1/2 cup chopped red onion

1/3 cup chopped green onions (4 medium)

1 cup French dressing

1 large tomato, chopped (1 cup)

1 medium green bell pepper, chopped (1 cup)

4 to 6 drops red pepper sauce

1 can (15 to 16 ounces) garbanzo beans, rinsed and drained

1 can (15 to 16 ounces) great northern beans, rinsed and drained

1 can (15 to 16 ounces) kidney beans, rinsed and drained

Cook and drain pasta as directed on package. Rinse with cold water; drain.

Mix pasta and remaining ingredients in large glass or plastic bowl. Cover and refrigerate at least 2 hours to blend flavors. Toss before serving.

1 Serving: Calories 385 (Calories from Fat 135); Fat 15g (Saturated 3g); Cholesterol 20mg; Sodium 810mg; Carbohydrate 57g (Dietary Fiber 9g); Protein 15g.

GARDEN GAZPACHO PASTA SALAD

8 SERVINGS

A summer salad that's perfect when your garden— or the farmers' market—is overflowing with tomatoes and zucchini.

1 1/2 cups uncooked rotini pasta (4 1/2 ounces)

1 1/2 cups shredded Cheddar cheese (6 ounces)

1/2 cup sliced ripe olives

1 1/2 cups salsa

2 tablespoons vegetable oil

2 small zucchini, sliced

1 large tomato, chopped (1 cup)

1 can (11 ounces) whole kernel corn, drained

Cook and drain pasta as directed on package. Rinse with cold water; drain.

Toss pasta and remaining ingredients in large glass or plastic bowl. Serve immediately, or cover and refrigerate up to 24 hours. Toss before serving.

1 Serving: Calories 270 (Calories from Fat 115); Fat 13g (Saturated 5g); Cholesterol 20mg; Sodium 630mg; Carbohydrate 31g (Dietary Fiber 3g); Protein 10g.

TOASTING NUTS

Aromatic, fragrant, toasty, crunchy and delicious are just a few of the words that describe toasted nuts. The addition of toasted nuts to pasta dishes offers delightful new flavors and textures.

Two toasting methods are described below. Start with fresh-tasting nuts that are whole, chopped, slivered or sliced. Smaller and thinner nuts will toast more quickly, as will those that contain more oil, such as pine nuts. Watch nuts carefully to avoid overbrowning or burning. Once toasted and completely cooled, nuts can be stored in a tightly covered container and refrigerated up to four months or frozen up to six months.

TO TOAST NUTS:

1. **Skillet Method:** Sprinkle up to 1/2 cup nuts in ungreased heavy skillet. Cook over medium-low heat 5 to 7 minutes, stirring frequently until browning begins, then stir nuts constantly until they are light golden brown. (Watch carefully; time varies greatly between gas and electric ranges.)

2. **Oven Method:** Heat oven to 350°. Spread nuts evenly in ungreased pan, stirring occasionally, until light golden brown, about 7 to 10 minutes. Smaller amounts of nuts may take less time and larger amounts more time.

USING TOASTED NUTS:

Toasted nuts taste particularly good in recipes that contain cream or those that use bold, assertive ingredients such as pesto or sun-dried tomatoes. While we've listed some suggestions below, you can also try creating your own new, exciting combinations!

- Toss pasta with whipping cream and crumbled gorgonzola or blue cheese; sprinkle with toasted walnuts and freshly ground pepper.

- Toss pasta with pesto, chopped tomatoes and sliced ripe olives; sprinkle with toasted pine nuts.

- Toss pasta with cooked chicken, Alfredo sauce, chopped artichoke hearts and red pepper strips; sprinkle with toasted pecans.

- Toss pasta with stir-fry sauce, cooked pork, broccoli, sliced carrots, pea pods and green onions; sprinkle with toasted almonds.

VEGETABLE-COUSCOUS SALAD

6 SERVINGS

2 cups chicken broth

1 1/2 cups uncooked couscous

1/2 cup pesto

3 tablespoons lemon juice

1/8 teaspoon pepper

1 medium tomato, chopped (3/4 cup)

2 green onions, thinly sliced

1 can (15 to 16 ounces) kidney beans, rinsed and drained

1 can (8 ounces) garbanzo beans, rinsed and drained

4 cups broccoli flowerets

Heat broth to boiling in 2-quart saucepan. Stir in couscous; remove from heat. Cover and let stand 5 minutes. Stir in remaining ingredients except broccoli. Serve over broccoli.

1 Serving: Calories 415 (Calories from Fat 135); Fat 15g (Saturated 3g); Cholesterol 5mg; Sodium 660mg; Carbohydrate 61g (Dietary Fiber 9g); Protein 18g.

GREEK PASTA SALAD

6 SERVINGS

4 cups cooked rosamarina (orzo) pasta

2 cups thinly sliced cucumber

1/4 cup finely chopped fresh parsley

1/4 cup olive or vegetable oil

1/4 cup lemon juice

1/4 teaspoon salt

1 medium tomato, chopped (3/4 cup)

1 small green bell pepper, chopped (1/2 cup)

1 small red onion, chopped

1 can (15 to 16 ounces) garbanzo beans,
    rinsed and drained

1 can (4 to 4 1/4 ounces) sliced ripe olives,
    drained

1/2 cup crumbled feta cheese

Mix all ingredients except cheese in glass or plastic bowl. Cover and refrigerate at least 1 hour to blend flavors. Top with cheese.

1 Serving: Calories 340 (Calories from Fat 135); Fat 15g (Saturated 4g); Cholesterol 10mg; Sodium 500mg; Carbohydrate 45g (Dietary Fiber 5g); Protein 11g.

HELPFUL NUTRITION AND COOKING INFORMATION

NUTRITION GUIDELINES:

Daily Values are set by the Food and Drug Administration and are based on the needs of most healthy adults. Percent Daily Values are based on an average diet of 2,000 calories per day. Your daily values may be higher or lower depending on your calorie needs.

Recommended intake for a daily diet of 2,000 calories:

Total Fat	Less than 65 g
Saturated Fat	Less than 20g
Cholesterol	Less than 300mg
Sodium	Less than 2,400mg
Total Carbohydrate	300g
Dietary Fiber	25g

CRITERIA USED FOR CALCULATING NUTRITION INFORMATION:

- The first ingredient is used wherever a choice is given (such as 1/3 cup sour cream or plain yogurt).

- The first ingredient amount is used wherever a range is given (such as 2 to 3 teaspoons milk).

- The first serving number is used wherever a range is given (such as 4 to 6 servings).

- "If desired" ingredients are not included, whether mentioned in the ingredient list or in the recipe directions as a suggestion (such as sprinkle with brown sugar if desired).

- Only the amount of a marinade of frying oil that is absorbed during preparation is calculated.

COOKING TERMS GLOSSARY:

Beat: Make smooth with a vigorous stirring motion using a spoon, wire whisk, egg beater or electric mixer.

Boil: Heat liquid until bubbles keep rising and breaking on the surface.

Chop: Cut food into small, uneven pieces; a sharp knife, food chopper or food processor may be used.

Core: Cut out the stem end and remove the seeds.

Cut in: Mix fat into a flour mixture with a pastry blender with a rolling motion or cutting with a fork or two knives until particles are size specified.

Dice: Cut into cubes smaller than 1/2 inch.

Drain: Pour off liquid or let it run off through the holes in a strainer or colander, as when draining cooked pasta or ground beef. Or, remove pieces of food from a fat or liquid and set them on paper towels to soak up excess moisture.

Flute: Flatten pastry evenly on rim of pie plate and press firmly around rim with tines of fork.

Grate: Rub against small holes of grater to cut into tiny pieces.

Grease: Spread the bottoms and side of a disk or pan with solid vegetable shortening using a pastry brush or paper towel.

Knead: Curve your fingers and fold dough toward you, then push it away with the heels of your hands, using a quick rocking motion.

Mix: Combine to distribute ingredients evenly using a spoon, fork, blender or an electric mixer.

Peel: Cut off the skin with a knife or peel with fingers.

Pipe: Press out frosting from a decorating bag using steady pressure to form a design or write a message. To finish a design, stop the pressure and lift the pint up and away.

Roll or **Pat:** Flatten and spread with a floured rolling pin or hands.

INGREDIENTS USED IN RECIPE TESTING AND NUTRITION CALCULATIONS:

- Large eggs, canned ready-to-use chicken broth, 2% milk, 80%-lean ground beef and vegetable-oil spread with less than 80% fat. These are used as they are the most commonly purchased ingredients within those categories.

- Regular long-grain white rice wherever cooked rice is listed, unless indicated.

- Nonfat, low-fat or low-sodium products are not used, unless indicated.

- Solid vegetable shortening (not margarine, butter and nonstick cooking sprays, as they can cause sticking problems) is used to grease pans, unless indicated.

EQUIPMENT USED IN RECIPE TESTING:

- Cookware and bakeware *without* nonstick coatings are used, unless indicated.

- Wherever a baking *pan* is specified in a recipe, a *metal* pan is used; wherever a baking *dish* or pie *plate* is specified, ovenproof *glass* or *ceramic* ovenware is used.

- A portable electric hand mixer is used for mixing *only when mixer speeds are specified* in the recipe directions.

METRIC CONVERSION GUIDE

VOLUME

U.S. Units	Canadian Metric	Australian Metric
1/4 teaspoon	1 mL	1 ml
1/2 teaspoon	2 mL	2 ml
1 teaspoon	5 mL	5 ml
1 tablespoon	15 mL	20 ml
1/4 cup	50 mL	60 ml
1/3 cup	75 mL	80 ml
1/2 cup	125 mL	125 ml
2/3 cup	150 mL	170 ml
3/4 cup	175 mL	190 ml
1 cup	250 mL	250 ml
1 quart	1 liter	1 liter
1 1/2 quarts	1.5 liters	1.5 liters
2 quarts	2 liters	2 liters
2 1/2 quarts	2.5 liters	2.5 liters
3 quarts	3 liters	3 liters
4 quarts	4 liters	4 liters

MEASUREMENTS

Inches	Centimeters
1	2.5
2	5.0
3	7.5
4	10.0
5	12.5
6	15.0
7	17.5
8	20.5
9	23.0
10	25.5
11	28.0
12	30.5
13	33.0
14	35.5
15	38.0

WEIGHT

U.S. Units	Canadian Metric	Australian Metric
1 ounce	30 grams	30 grams
2 ounces	55 grams	60 grams
3 ounces	85 grams	90 grams
4 ounces (1/4 pound)	115 grams	125 grams
8 ounces (1/2 pound)	225 grams	225 grams
16 ounces (1 pound)	455 grams	500 grams
1 pound	455 grams	1/2 kilogram

TEMPERATURES

Fahrenheit	Celsius
32°	0°
212°	100°
250°	120°
275°	140°
300°	150°
325°	160°
350°	180°
375°	190°
400°	200°
425°	220°
450°	230°
475°	240°
500°	260°

Note: The recipes in this cookbook have not been developed or tested using metric measures. When converting recipes to metric, some variations in quality may be noted.

𝒥NDEX

Numbers in *italics* refer to photos.